LOUISE

AUTOBIOGRAPHICAL PRINTS

BOURGEOIS

Introduction

Roger Malbert

When Louise Bourgeois died in 2010 at the age of 98, she was such a towering presence in the contemporary art world that it is easy to forget that it was not until the early 1980s, when she was in her seventies, that she achieved international renown. Her striking face is best known from photographs of her in old age, notably Robert Mapplethorpe's famous 1982 image of her grinning mischievously and cradling her bronze sculpture of a giant phallus. Her retrospective at the Museum of Modern Art in New York in the same year turned out to be a mid-career survey; it was followed by nearly three decades of astonishing creativity, during which she produced many of her most powerful and original works.

The evolution of Louise Bourgeois' career as a sculptor can be charted in roughly demarcated phases: the totemic stick-like wooden personages of the late 1940s; the vertically stacked segments and spirals of the early 1950s; the plaster 'lairs' and bulbous or pendulous forms in plaster or poured latex of the 1960s and '70s; the phallic and breast-like marbles and bronzes of the 1980s; the giant spider in steel and bronze of the late 1990s; the stitched fabric figures and heads and the assemblage-interiors – the 'Cells' – of the final two decades. By contrast, her drawings, prints and watercolours run a more continuous course, with both style and imagery recurring over decades. Although her activity in printmaking is intermittent – starting in 1939 after her move to New York but with an interval of more than 25 years from 1947 – images are often derived from drawings of earlier periods: for example,

Untitled (Birth) (p. 55) from the *Autobiographical Series* of 1994 is exactly transcribed from a drawing the artist made in 1941; another drypoint, *Self Portrait*, 1993, similarly transcribes a drawing of 1942; and the iconic *Femme Maison*, a naked woman 'wearing' a house, was produced as a photogravure in 1984 after a drawing of 1947.

Bourgeois' drawings are often interwoven with her writings: the *Insomnia Drawings* from 1994–95 (the same period as the *Autobiographical Series*) are intensely personal and self-revealing, recording her obsessions and fears in intimate journals that were evidently not intended, at the time of their creation, to see the light of day. And the posthumously published 'psychoanalytical writings', 1952–66,[1] provide insights into the mind of a uniquely self-aware and passionate artist who sought to 'short-circuit the conscious and to have direct access to deeper perceptions of the unconscious'. Bourgeois was steeped in psychoanalysis. In 1952, she entered into analysis with Dr Henry Lowenfeld, a left-wing Jewish German émigré with a particular interest in artists' creative processes, and she continued to see him, irregularly, until 1982. This was not unusual for artists in New York in the 1950s – several of the Abstract Expressionists achieved artistic breakthroughs with the help of analysis – but Bourgeois was exceptional in her profound intellectual engagement with psychoanalytic theory. She read widely, and even at one stage considered training as a child psychologist.

Sexuality, the body, motherhood and family relations are Bourgeois' predominant themes and they are rooted in her biography, especially in memories of early childhood. The violent emotions of infancy – aggression, jealous rage, fear of separation and abandonment – were primary sources of inspiration to which she consistently returned. To understand her obsessions it is necessary to know something of her life story.

Louise Bourgeois was born in Paris, the second daughter of parents who ran a tapestry restoration business. As a young girl, her talent for drawing was deployed in filling in the lost parts of figures in damaged tapestries, often where legs and feet had worn away. (The symbolic aspect of reparation and the role of scissors and needles as instruments associated with this largely feminine activity remained strongly evocative for her.) When she was 11, her father introduced a young woman into the home, ostensibly to teach English to her and her younger brother Pierre. In fact, Sadie was his mistress and this flagrant infidelity and disruption of family life had a traumatic effect on Louise, who refers to it repeatedly as an overwhelming and defining experience. Her anger towards her father – whom she resembled in looks and temperament – was to be one of the driving forces in her imaginative life. She was extremely close to her mother, who had been unwell since contracting Spanish flu at the end of the First World War. After she died in 1932, the heartbroken Louise enrolled in the Sorbonne, taking courses in solid geometry and differential calculus until February 1933, when she gave up the study of mathematics for art. In 1938 she briefly ran a gallery selling prints in her father's showroom, and there she met Robert Goldwater, an American art historian specialising in tribal art. They married and sailed to New York that same year.

Given her preoccupation with the unconscious, Bourgeois might be presumed to be a child of surrealism, but she spoke dismissively of the surrealists, who had evidently ignored her when she encountered them in Paris. They were not interested in women, she said, unless they were rich. When André Breton and Marcel Duchamp turned up in New York, she 'objected...violently to their pontifications. Since I was a runaway, father figures on these shores rubbed me up the wrong way.'[2]

In New York, Bourgeois enrolled in the Art Students League and studied painting and lithography. Meanwhile she and her husband were raising three sons, one adopted in 1939, followed by two born to her in 1940 and '41. He was a feminist and a calm, devoted father: she never saw him angry, she said – and the same had been true of her mother. A print in the *Autobiographical Series* showing two children in the bath recalls these years (p. 58). Bourgeois said of this image: 'This is the bathroom at 18th Street. Everything is exactly the same... the cabinet... the tub with feet... it is very accurate... It was really something to have three children and also try to work. It was a lot of physical work. I could never carry a child, even when they were very little... I had to have ways to hoist them. So here they help each other. They are happy... it is very tender.'[3]

During the early 1940s Bourgeois worked on prints at home, having acquired an intaglio press. After the war, she enrolled at S.W. Hayter's print workshop, Atelier 17, and in 1947 she produced a key work, *He Disappeared into Complete Silence*, a book of nine engravings, accompanied by short parables written by the artist. The techniques of engraving and drypoint involve incising a copper plate with a steel burin or needle, as opposed to etching, which requires acid. The physical act of cutting into the plate appealed to Bourgeois, as more sculptural and expressive, and perhaps more aggressive. The solitary towers and ladders in these images clearly represent human estrangement. They anticipate the tall wooden personages or 'effigies' that Bourgeois now began to carve, signalling a decisive shift from printmaking to sculpture. She would not return to printmaking with any seriousness until the 1980s, but when she did, it was to those same techniques, and using the same press at home. However, her interest in graphic art found expression in another way when in 1956 she opened a shop, Erasmus Books and Prints, a short-lived commercial experiment.

Bourgeois' father died in 1951, but this did not resolve her struggle with the tyrannical, self-aggrandising 'macho father figure'; he remained the object of her enmity and ridicule for almost 60 more years. In 1974 – the year after the sudden death of her husband Robert – she presented the first of her large-scale sculptural installations, *The Destruction of the Father*, a symbolic dinner party made of wood, plaster, fabric and latex, in which the bodily parts of the father are dismembered and laid out to be devoured by his children in an act of supreme revenge.

The purpose of this work, she later said, was to exorcise fear: 'And after it was shown... I felt like a different person. Now, I don't want to use the word *thérapeutique*, but an exorcism is a therapeutic venture. So the reason for making this work was catharsis.'[4]

Compared to the visceral and symbolic impact of her sculptures and installations, the imagery of the *Autobiographical Series* seems remarkably tame, consisting mostly of quiet, literal depictions of figures in interiors. Yet, even the most cursorily drawn of them represents a moment charged with emotional significance. Bourgeois spoke of her realist drawings as crucially 'anchored in place and time. They depend on the accuracy of memory'. Hence her account of the children in the bath; and of another bathroom scene, showing a woman washing her long hair (p. 62): 'This is a girlhood memory... this is about beautiful hair, of course... The little face looking in... he is not laughing at her... because she is beautiful. But he cannot pull a fast one on anybody... his face is registered there in the mirror!'[5] In another image (p. 66), a man wearing a coat – presumably Robert – is sleeping in a chair, also watched by a face at the window. Another print (p. 57) on which the artist's comments are recorded – where aquatint offsets the starkly scratched line – shows a woman reaching up to adjust the hands of a grandfather clock. Bourgeois recalled that as a child it was her task to wind up the clock. And her further remarks illustrate her elaborate association of ideas connected with ostensibly simple subjects: '... to rewind is to make a spiral. And the action demonstrates that even though time is unlimited, there is a limit to how much you can put on it. As you are tightening the spiral you must take care. If you tighten too much you risk breaking it. It is the same with sewing. Sewing without a knot at the end of the thread is not sewing. I am consistent in my spiral. For me there is no break. There is never an interruption in the spiral because I cannot stand interruptions.'[6]

Only two prints in the *Autobiographical Series* were given titles by the artist, and both deal with parenthood: *Empty Nest* (p. 59) shows a woman perched on a stool weeping, presumably missing her absent children; *Paternity* (p. 65) depicts a father feeding his infant child. The image of a woman carrying a suitcase (p. 60) is also perhaps related to anxieties surrounding parenthood. Bourgeois wrote on the back of one impression, 'Robert did not want children. I did. It was a very serious episode. I thought we couldn't have a child. If we did not adopt a child, I am leaving. When they were there… He loved them + I lost interest.'[7] *Untitled* (Birth) of a child emerging from his mother, enveloped in her long hair, repudiates that fear of infertility (p. 55); and *Untitled* (Scissors) shows two pairs of scissors, the smaller suspended by a thread – an umbilical cord – from the larger (p. 54). These two more strenuous images are closer to the drypoints; they are imaginative inventions rather than literal memories. Six of the drypoints are encircled by black, evoking the darkness of night; they invite interpretation as metaphors or dreams. There is a primitive edge in the fierce directness and grotesque humour of the tongue in *Madeleine* (p. 30), for example, or the feet in feet in *The Smell of the Feet* (p. 46), that is reminiscent of *art brut* or children's art. Yet these are mature works by one of the greatest artists of the late twentieth century. Bourgeois' ability to regress, to mine the depths of her unconscious while maintaining her poise as a sophisticated and lauded public figure, was an extraordinary gift, of which she was well aware. 'Art is a privilege, a blessing, a relief', she said. 'It is a fantastic privilege to have access to the unconscious... I had to be worthy of this privilege, and to exercise it. It was a privilege also to be able to sublimate... There is something very special in being able to sublimate your unconscious, and something very painful in the access to it. But there is no escape from it, and no escape from access once it is given to you, once you are favoured with it, whether you want it or not.'[8]

1 Louise Bourgeois, *The Return of the Repressed*, ed. Philip Larratt-Smith (London: Violette Editions, 2012)
2 Quoted in Rainer Crone and Petrus Graf Schaesberg (eds.), *Louise Bourgeois: The Secret of the Cells* (Munich, New York and London: Prestel, 2008), p. 35
3 Carol Smith and Deborah Wye, *The Prints of Louise Bourgeois* (New York: The Museum of Modern Art, 1994), p. 234
4 Louise Bourgeois, *Destruction of the Father Reconstruction of the Father, Writings and Interviews 1923–1997*, ed. Marie-Laure Bernadac and Hans-Ulrich Obrist (Cambridge Mass: MIT Press, 2008), p. 158
5 Smith and Wye 1994, p. 233
6 Quoted in 'Paulo Herkenhoff in conversation with Louise Bourgeois, transcribed and edited by Thyrza Nichols Goodeve', in Robert Storr, Paulo Herkenhoff, Allan Schwartzman (eds.), *Louise Bourgeois* (London: Phaidon, 2003), p. 12
7 Inscribed on verso of state 1, quoted in Cat. No. 436/11 of *Louise Bourgeois, The Complete Prints & Books*: Museum of Modern Art website: http://www.moma.org/explore/collection/lb/index
8 Bourgeois, *Destruction of the Father. . .*, p. 164

Bourgeois' Prints: A Psychoanalyst's View

Juliet Mitchell

Throughout the extraordinary private notes she made during her very long analysis with Dr Henry Lowenfeld, a refugee Freudian in New York with an interest in art,[1] Louise Bourgeois noted time and again her terrible fear of collapsing with a nervous breakdown. In a posthumously published, unfinished article 'A Fear of Breakdown',[2] psychoanalyst Donald Winnicott (whose work Bourgeois knew) claimed that this probably universal fear referred to a future which, unbeknownst to the person concerned, had already happened in the distant infantile past.

What is feared is the agonising experience of a major trauma that occurred when, because of the immaturity of the infant's ego, there was no recourse to a story or narrative about its life. The adult patient comes to therapy to tell a story but this story unwittingly hides the dread of a collapse into an earlier psychosis or madness. Because the trauma that is feared is unknown, to explore it would feel like having the breakdown here and now. Louise Bourgeois' two sets of prints, the *Autobiographical Series* from 1994 and the *11 Drypoints* from 1999, are chronologically out of order: the *Autobiographical Series* is the later story, which she tells first. The drypoints, created five years later, refer mainly to her earlier infancy and childhood, suggesting that the drypoints, but not the autobiographical prints, are touching the fear of a future breakdown that in fact happened in infancy. As explored below, the order in which the series were created is telling.

What is the early 'breakdown' referred to here? Winnicott claims that in the 'terrible twos' and 'dreadful threes' the toddler suffers a 'trauma of separation' from the mother. I have argued that this is also a 'sibling trauma'. The toddler becomes yesterday's baby when a new baby (actual or expected) steals this identity. The toddler temporarily breaks down, ragingly protesting the experience of the annihilation of the immature ego by this apparent replacement. Bourgeois links her terror of breakdown to her complex relationship with the sad history of her younger brother: he suffered a breakdown in 1945, and now it is she, a toddler at the time of his birth, who dreads the same fate.[3] Although no one wants the emergence of the psychotic/mad experience of this early trauma, Bourgeois (and Winnicott) knew it must be confronted. Psychoanalysis is a 'talking cure'; art, a visual practice. The toddler is positioned where speaking is still seeing; seeing, speaking. Bourgeois also conflates these processes.

Bourgeois said 'art is a language', with a tongue-in-cheek reference to psychoanalyst Jacques Lacan's dictum: 'the unconscious is structured like a language'. This suggests an equation between the two practices: what the psychoanalyst and clinical patient try to understand, Bourgeois *makes*. Because of this equation, Bourgeois, embedded as she was within psychoanalysis, did not want us to *interpret* her work as one expertise addressing another. Instead we should see that there is an 'elective affinity' between the process of psychoanalysis and the work of art. As therapist and patient give each other their responses (the therapist's 'free attention' and the patient's 'free associations'), so artwork and spectator should respond to each other, the artwork being attentively there to allow the viewer to see and say what may previously have been unconscious.

The concepts and practices of the verbal-visual, that is, the 'literal', the 'metaphor', the 'self-portrait' and the 'narrative', are the well-trodden shared terrain of psychoanalysis and Bourgeois' art. The small child – still very alive in the adult – who is being recaptured in the clinical encounter and in these prints initially only has access to the linguistically and visually literal. I recall (and, in my mind's eye, see) a charming tableau recounted by the psychoanalyst Wilfred Bion in which a mother goes into the bedroom to find her daughter with her cheek against the baby's tummy – she is 'keeping an eye on the baby'. After this presentation of herself comes the use of metaphor and with this the growing ability for a self-*re*presentation, a 'self-portrait', and a story about the self. When the story enters the terrain of a shared human experience, it can become a narrative: an autobiography is just such a story.

The well-known narrative for anyone interested in psychoanalysis is the story of Oedipus' love for his mother and the threat of castration if he indulges it (as Oedipus did). There is a girl's version of Oedipus that Bourgeois forefronts. Her public 'psychoanalytic' pronouncements (different from her private, now archival jottings) tell the story of her personal experience of child-abuse from her father and her tutor (his mistress), and her mother's collusion. She made this a feminist narrative that could join the meta-psychological Oedipus story – a narrative that belongs to every woman whatever the personal differences. But what people also all have in common is that not one of us perfectly resolves the Oedipus complex; hopefully, both clinical practice and Bourgeois' art practice will help us find a richer, more widely human narrative than the limited story with which we started. However, the very different and earlier separation/sibling trauma had not yet got a story, let alone a narrative. Thus, in these print-works Bourgeois may be using the Oedipal *Autobiographical Series* as a way of delaying what she dreads – her fear of the crisis that had already happened when she was 13 months old and her brother was born. This earlier episode features later, in the drypoints.

When the small child moves forward from literal thinking to using metaphors, this is entirely normative, age appropriate. However, when in the clinic or while art-making, the adult retraces the historic breakdown that must be faced, the portals of madness are opened up, the metaphor is lost and the literal becomes what is known as the psychotic 'concrete'. This is why somewhere we all fear the breakdown. However, the clinical practice and the work of art contain it, hopefully offering a safe haven where the 'scream' can be heard and seen.

The prints partially masquerade as children's drawings. Yet, although Bourgeois calls drypoint scratching 'endearing', no child could score the etching plate in this way. Because of the return journey from the adult's fear to the toddler's unknown experience, the terrifying, the agony, always lurks. But because of the child's forward march, the literal and the metaphoric can be played and laughed with. Bourgeois' people are young and old in feeling at the same time: the psychoanalyst and Bourgeois move backwards with the adult into the frightening, and forward with the child who, after finding their own literalness playful and humorous, can turn it into shared jokes, and represent it as puns, visual and verbal.

Recalling the little girl with her eye on the baby, we can see that Bourgeois sprinkles eyes over many of her works; she knows that eyes cannot lie or, if they lie, you can *see* the lie. The eyes of *The Angry Cat* (p. 50) are fearful behind its anger – they are the strongest element of this drypoint – but this bejewelled cat is funny too. At first I found myself somewhat unnerved by feeling irritated at the fences connecting, as thin lines, four non-identical but so-alike houses in *Fences Are Obsolete* (p. 32). To counter my irritation I recalled my daughter when tiny, jumping with intense concentration from side to side of a long row of wooden bricks she had arranged. In my pleasurable memory, she told me she was 'fencing', as she imagined the sport her babysitter had left her to practise. Was I irritated because these 'dead' blank-face houses that I felt should hold the 'ego' have weak (de)fences? Was this 'divided self', this split ego, only linked by very faint psychic (de)fences? Winnicott wrote:

> [...] what we see clinically is always a *defence* organisation, even in the autism of childhood schizophrenia.

> The underlying agony is unthinkable. [...] psychotic illness is a *defence* organisation relative to a primitive agency.[4]

The play on garden fence and defence mechanism in *Fences Are Obsolete* is not unusual: Bourgeois loves to pun. Is it too much of a stretch to see the cat's face in *The Angry Cat* as '*chat*erred', and therefore in need of the glass of wine which forms her mouth and nose? Probably – but nonetheless, the combination of horror and humour in animal form is a major achievement of this work. As the infant-becoming-a-child loves to listen to stories about animals who are people and vice-versa, it also begins to perceive itself. If that other one is the baby whom my mother cuddles, then there is also a story about me – Louise – angry cat or little girl growing up. This toddler often starts this self-as-other-as-object by using its own name and 'me' precedes 'I'. This is the moment of the emergence of the self-portrait.

A self-portrait lurks within several of the drypoints. These self-portraits do not form a sequence and can be taken in any order. Unlike narrative time, psychic time does not have a beginning, a middle and an end. The notion of 'object-relations' in psychoanalysis indicates that the child becomes attracted and attached to a person or part of the person. Instead, we should see that objects come helter-skelter at the baby, infant and traumatised person. To get away from these besieging objects, the broken bits of ego put up a number of earlier pre-Oedipal strategies and defences. Some of these, so vivid in Bourgeois' work, include 'falling forever', a device of 'self-holding operation' (as seen in her many spiral sculptures); narcissism, an effort to hold the ego pieces together; omnipotence, to be all-powerful enough to look after the abandoned self – all these evince a desperate wish for what one needs. Thus a fearful nasty mosquito becomes a fairy princess (*Mosquito*, p. 44). Anthropomorphising her wish to be a princess, Bourgeois allows the fairy to give birth to a replica of itself (although the tiny offspring is more like a scorpion). This is parthenogenesis – the process by which creatures have babies without fertilisation; in humans it is an imagined practice beloved of two- to three-year-old children who if asked where they get their many babies from, answer: 'from myself, of course'. (Like art?) In reality, mosquitoes do not reproduce like this: instead, they produce dangerous eggs.

There is also the defence provided by dissociation: has the girl-mother with the silly smile and precariously held jelly-baby doll with its prominent, ambiguous genitals in *Mother and Child* (p. 48) been thrown down the stairs? Or, more likely, does she realise it is too much to climb up and join the father/husband who has disappeared into total silence, a black box at the top?

In *Please Hang in There* (p. 38), Bourgeois' trademark long hair is hanging between perilous peaks as she stands in an impossible horizontal from the mountain-side. (Falling forever or ego-disintegration?) Again with a smile on her face, the Louise girl is assassinated by her older sister Henriette's crutch in *The Accident* (p. 40). From her own account in the diaries and archival notes, Bourgeois was murderously jealous of Henriette's teenage profligacy, followed by her trousseau-rich marriage. This self-portrait is of denial: one of the two of them is smiling inanely at being murdered or murdering. There may also be a reference here to the disabilities of French soldiers after the First World War: as a young woman, Louise was appalled beyond belief at the broken bodies of the soldiers employed in the basements of the Louvre where she also worked.

In *Fear* (p. 34) Louise holds on for dear life by the tips of her fingers in a large tent or capsule. In the topmost of three smaller tents she features as her much-portrayed cat, Champfleurette (a seductively flowery field),[5] in a form that recalls her explicitly bisexual sculpture *Janus Fleuri,* 1968, an acknowledged self-portrait. The person-cat is seductive. Seduction – the winsome ways of the two-year-old – is a feature of narcissism. As an adult, Bourgeois remarks in her notes how time and again she put 'her foot in it', so her mouth said the wrong thing with friends and foes alike. In her print *Don't Put Your Foot in Your Mouth* (p. 42) a small girl is made to do what only a baby can do – putting this same foot in her mouth: a metaphor expressed as a literal impossibility. Once one is no longer a baby, other people's feet tend only to smell and need to be sneezed or magicked away by one's starry thoughts (p. 46). From feet to socks (p. 36) – socks which are like standardised cheap Christmas stockings. Instead of presents, in a near hallucination which could tumble into a delusion, there are nasty painted or mouldy toenails coming through them. And so, central to Bourgeois' concern with the making of the past, will the '*temps perdu*' of Proust's masterpiece choke her? With the tight string of beads – the 'choker' – around her neck, she cannot swallow this lost past. Instead she will stick out her tongue at all who want to take it in, or are taken in by it (p. 30). Behind all these defences is 'the unthinkable'.

The self-portrait links the set of *11 Drypoints* to the *Autobiographical Series*. It comes at the psychological stage when the infant/child is still often other people, other animals. But as it underlies the narrative, it has only a subterranean existence. The public surface story that avoids and introduces the earlier state-of-affairs has a (sort of) beginning, a middle and an end. The narrative opens with the self-portrait of *Untitled* (Birth); giving birth and being born at the same time (p. 55). An intellectually vexed, thinking woman – a Louise – is giving birth to a head the same size as her own. Ideas are one thing, experience another: any parturient mother knows that the tiny head of the baby who is trying or (like Bourgeois' son, Alain) trying *not* to get out always *feels* immense. Turn the print around and the akimbo legs of the mother become the near foetal arms of a baby that indeed will be as big as the mother. Bourgeois' long hair, like a cowl, protects or entangles. This is not to *think* about the relationship of giving birth and of being born – it is to feel all the contradictions embedded there; my own body is churned up as it can be in a clinical session. I will think later.

As an artist, Bourgeois' ego can produce the ego-in-pieces, the immature ego as it would be in psychoanalytic sessions that tackled the fear of breakdown or fear of death. Those peeping in through small apertures in the *Autobiographical Series* may be bits of her own ego which are no different from mine or other people's. One of the little peeping heads has a tree beside it (p. 62) – her own head, the head of the father/husband, of paternity, of herself as husband/father? This is a father who holds almost in his lap a swaddled and therefore untouched baby while he dreams of it growing up, plant-like, near him — a kind and gentle portrait (p. 65). The two children in the bath (p. 58) are usually claimed as two of her sons. Perhaps, but the tub could also come from recollections of pre-war France when Bourgeois (then a short-haired child) had poked fun at her brother Pierre's penis.

Bourgeois depended on the annoying-endearing presence of her three sons as they were growing up; when they went away to summer camp she expressly described in her notes how she experienced empty nest syndrome, a very American notion, which militated against the work she had so craved to do in her children's absence. In *Empty Nest* (p. 59), Bourgeois does not have her feet on the ground – she sits on a three-legged stool (her three sons?), her two feet on a four-legged one (sons and husband/mother?). Is her head in her hands for the sadness of loss or to find new inspiration? In the 1990s, after members of her family had either left home or died prematurely, she in fact became more prolific than ever.

Bourgeois goes over the edge of the breakdown precipice and comes back carrying the ego's pieces. To me, however, one print is neither ideal nor a self-portrait, it is a portrait plain and simple: the boy and girl (p. 56). The full meaning of her brother Pierre's early death in 1960 had yet to arrive in her art at the end of the century. Before she gets there (see *Cell XIV (Portrait)* – two ears, one agony, her tragedy and his),

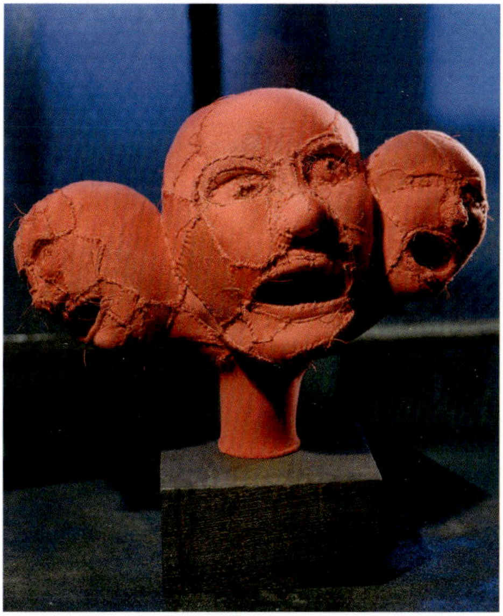

Louise Bourgeois
Cell XIV (Portrait), 2000 (detail)
Steel, glass, wood, metal and red fabric
187.9 × 121.9 × 121.9 cm
Artist Rooms Foundation

it is he not she who has turned his back and she who is left wondering anxiously/longingly about him.

This reverses an iconic photograph from 1917 in which Pierre is looking adoringly at Louise.

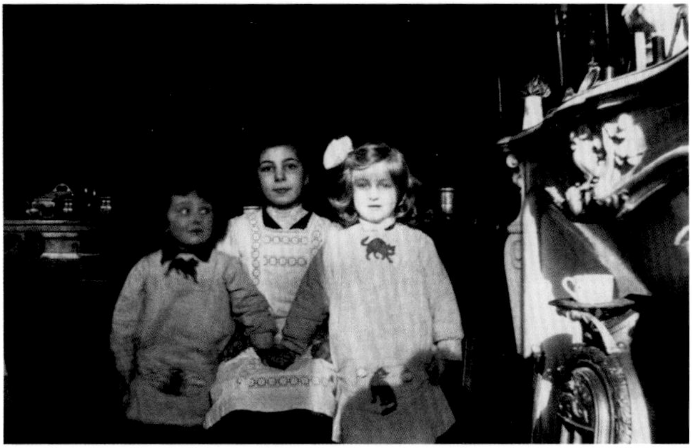

Louise Bourgeois (right) with her brother and her sister, circa 1917

Narrative, a notion over-worked by Louise and her critics (myself included), sorts out, almost codifies, the underlying simultaneity of emotions, of psychic defences. In the breakdown, the opposite poles of ambivalence momentarily lie together. The very structure of the narrative – angry and fearful, love and hate – are divided up and benignly split to facilitate social life. In her *Autobiographical Series* Bourgeois can enjoy and laugh at her portrayal of her own integrated self when she lives in her body (Winnicott calls this 'psychosomatic collusion') and relates to other people (object relating). But though the form has a beginning in birth and her family of origin, a middle in her family of orientation and an end, perhaps, in her walking away from both, all is not as easy as it seems. Past and present may structure but they cannot be separated, autobiography legitimates self-portraiture making it just more explicit. As would a child, Louise looks at her own reflection in the distorting curve of her large spoon from a small teacup (p. 67), then, very much an adult, she luxuriates in a bath where she can see simultaneously her real feet at the edge and her attractive pose reflected in a mirror (p. 63). Cutting scissors give birth to a smaller pair of testicles with an uncut umbilical attachment (p. 54). In infancy both genders imagine they can give birth and have both sexes' sexual organs – psychological bisexuality. But this is also a portrait of herself – 'like (seamstress) mother – like daughter' – dedicated to sewing (p. 61). Time passes, a hotelier rests his head on his arm while one o'clock rocks around the clock (p. 64); her father or husband lounges hat-on-head from the past (p. 66); she washes her flowing hair (p. 62) and stretches to turn the old-fashioned grandfather clock to 5pm, time for tea (p. 57). This is something of how I (here mostly a psychoanalyst) *respond* to Louise, who goes on making – and we can stay or leave, or come back to experience more. Of one thing we can be certain: Louise Bourgeois had psychoanalysis in her bloodstream.

1 This period of analysis was conducted most intensely between 1952 and 1966 but continued until 1982.
2 D. W. Winnicott, 'Fear of Breakdown', in *International Review of Psycho-analysis* 1 (1974), pp. 103–07
3 Juliet Mitchell, 'Love and Hate: Girl and Boy', in *London Review of Books*, vol. 36, no. 21
4 Ibid. (My italics)
5 *Champfleurette, the White Cat* (1993), MoMA, New York

11
Drypoints

Madeleine

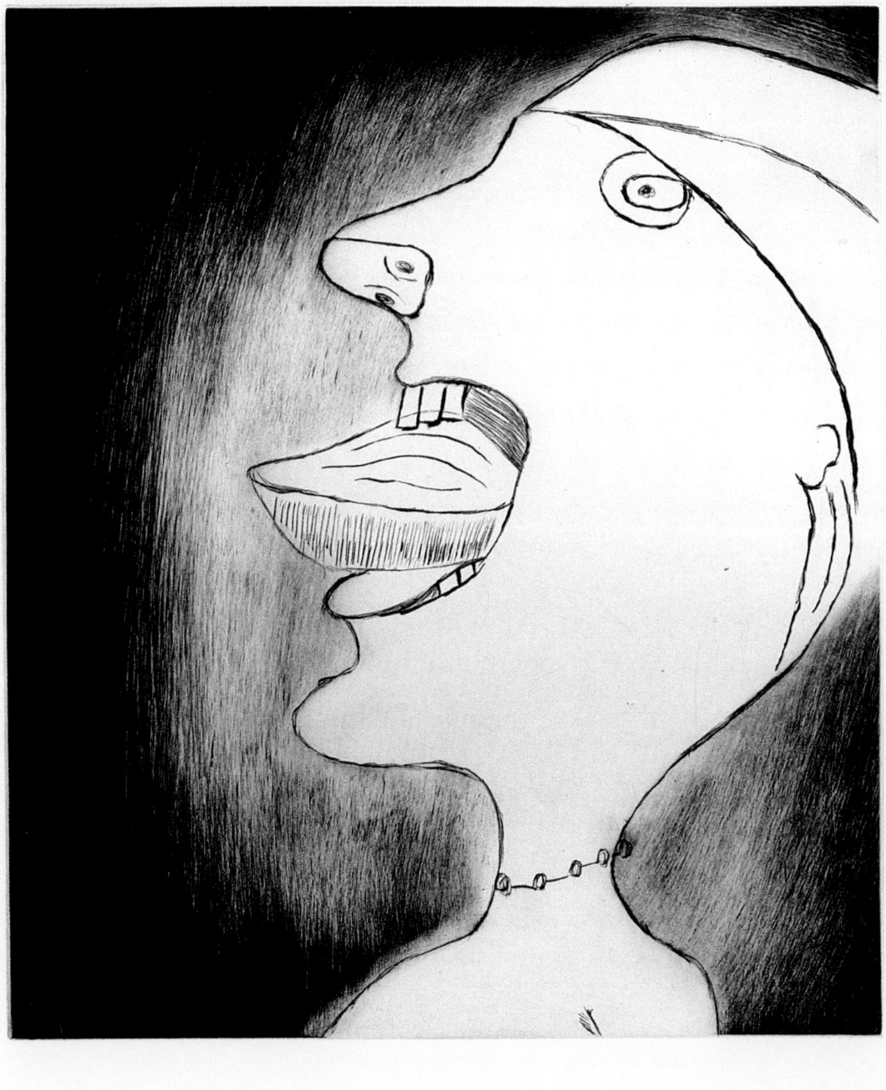

Fences Are Obsolete

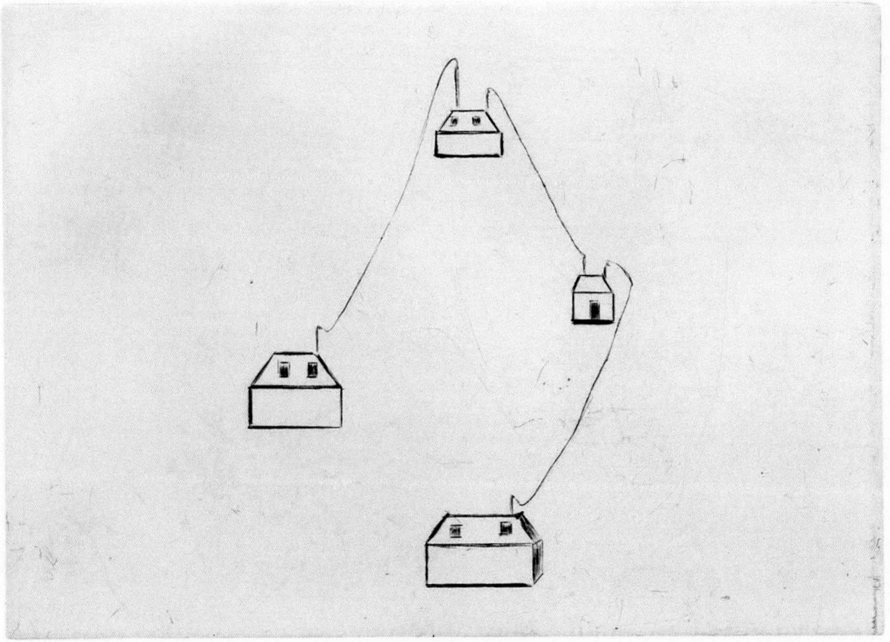

Fear

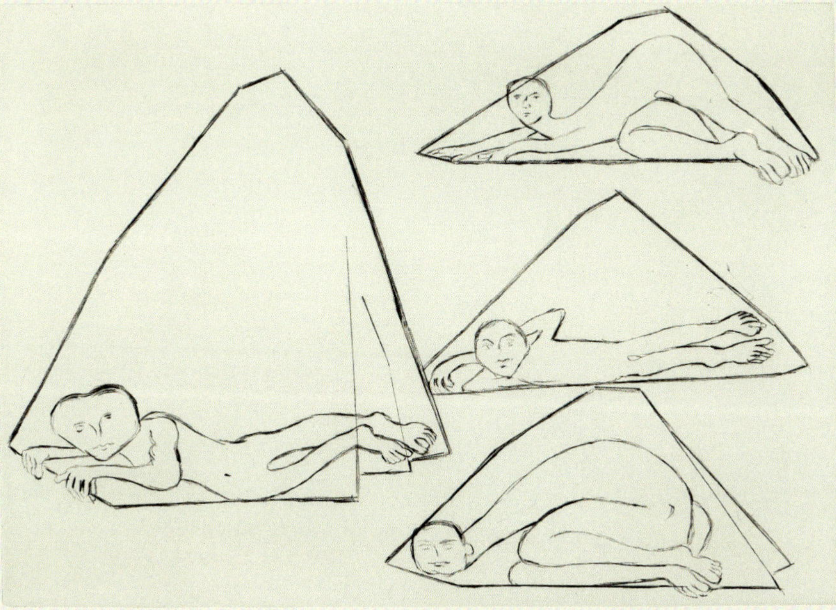

Feet (Socks)

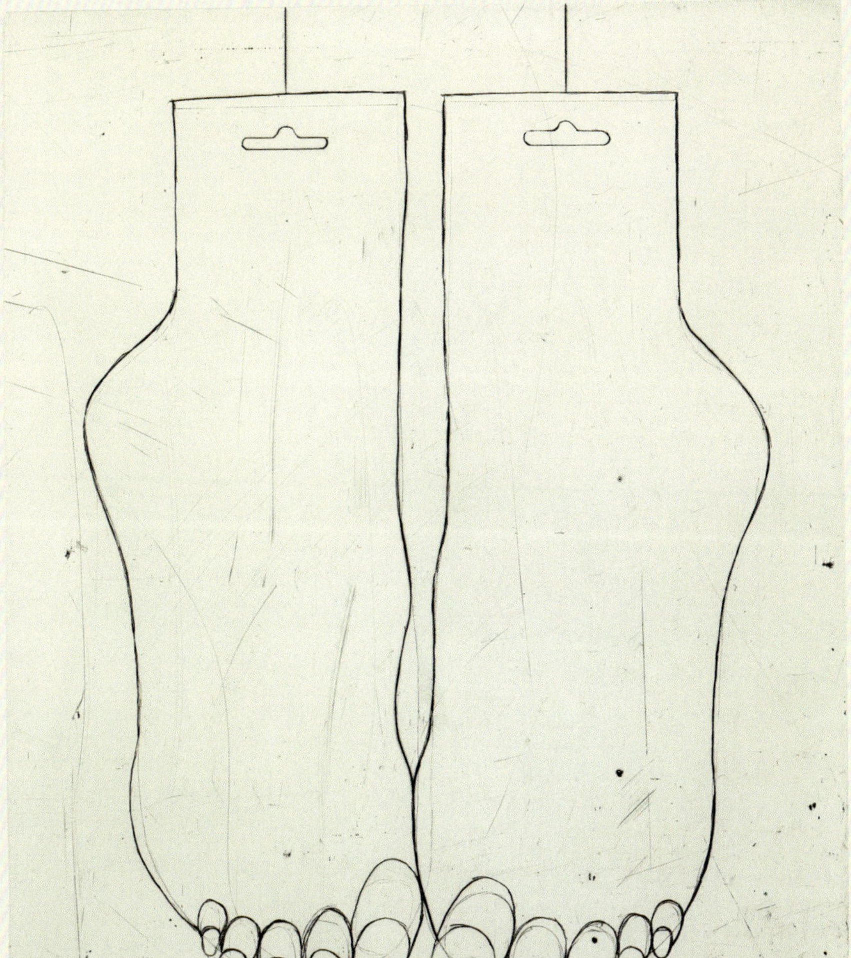

Please Hang in There

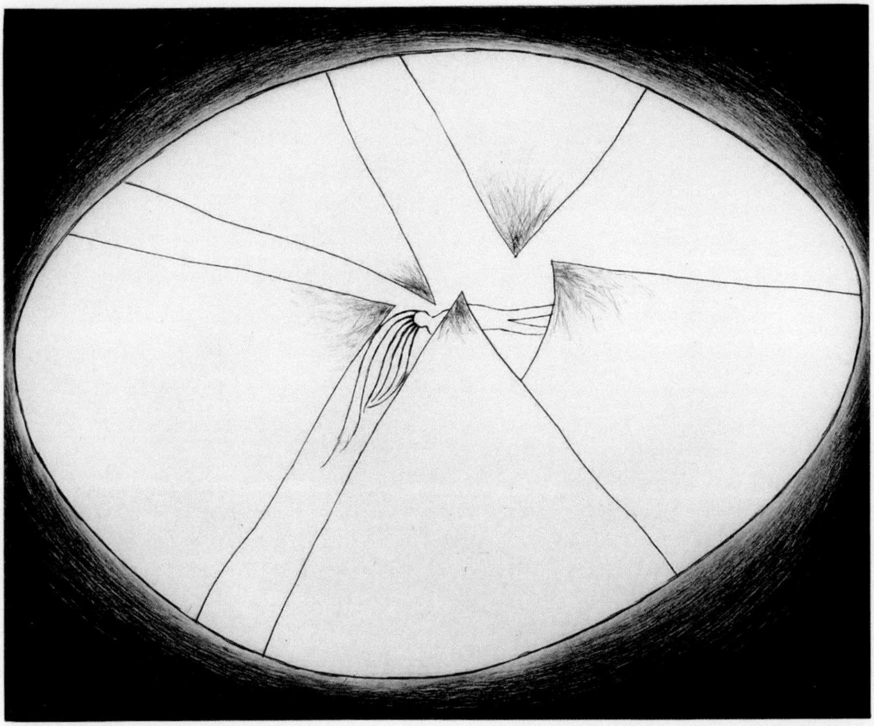

The Accident

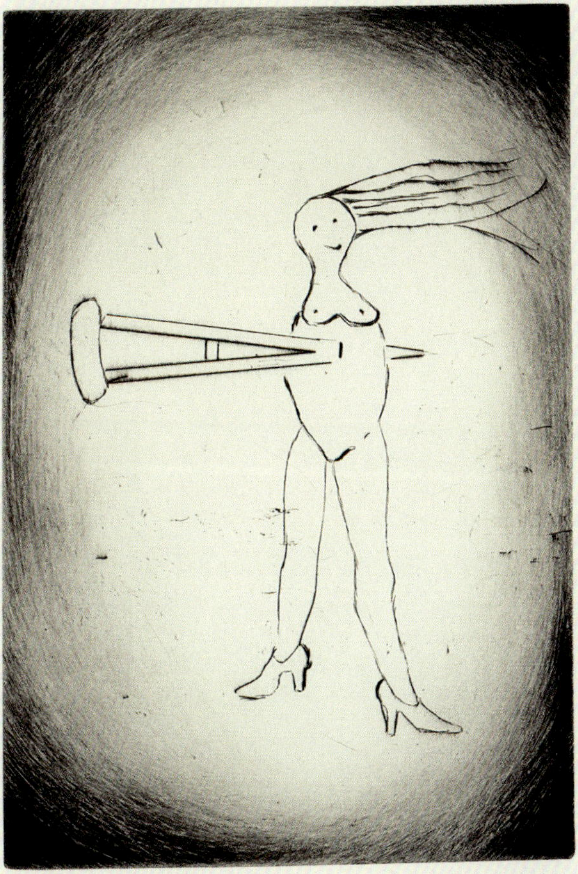

Don't Put Your Foot in Your Mouth

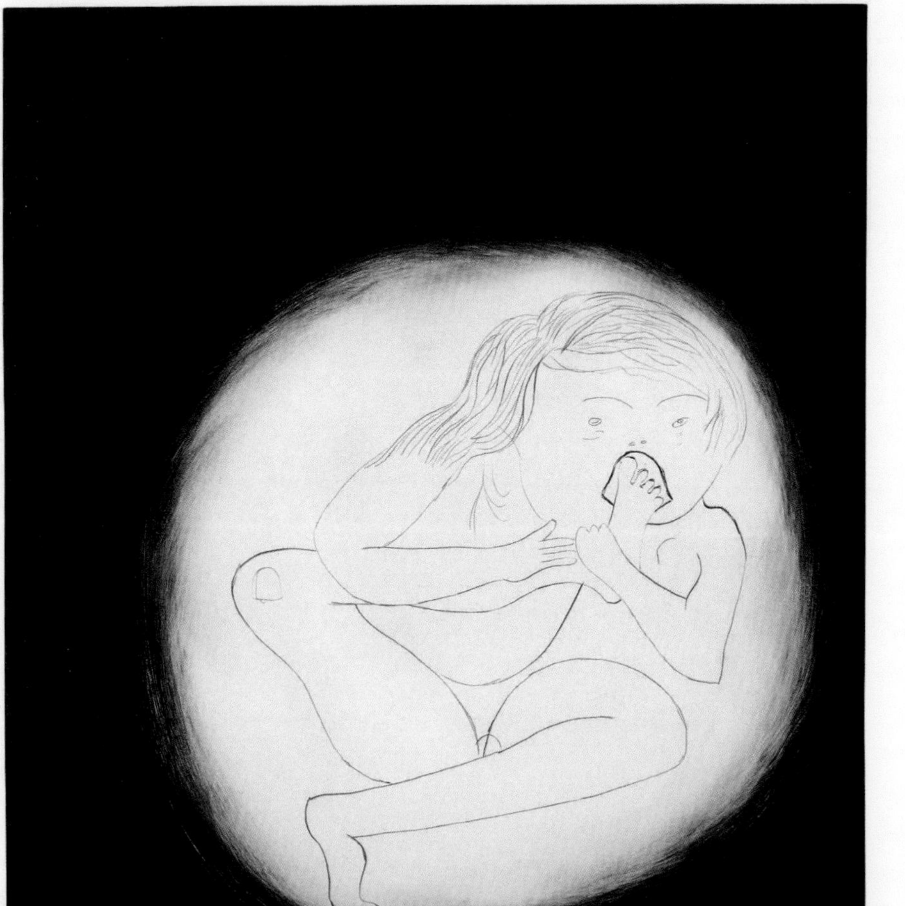

Mosquito

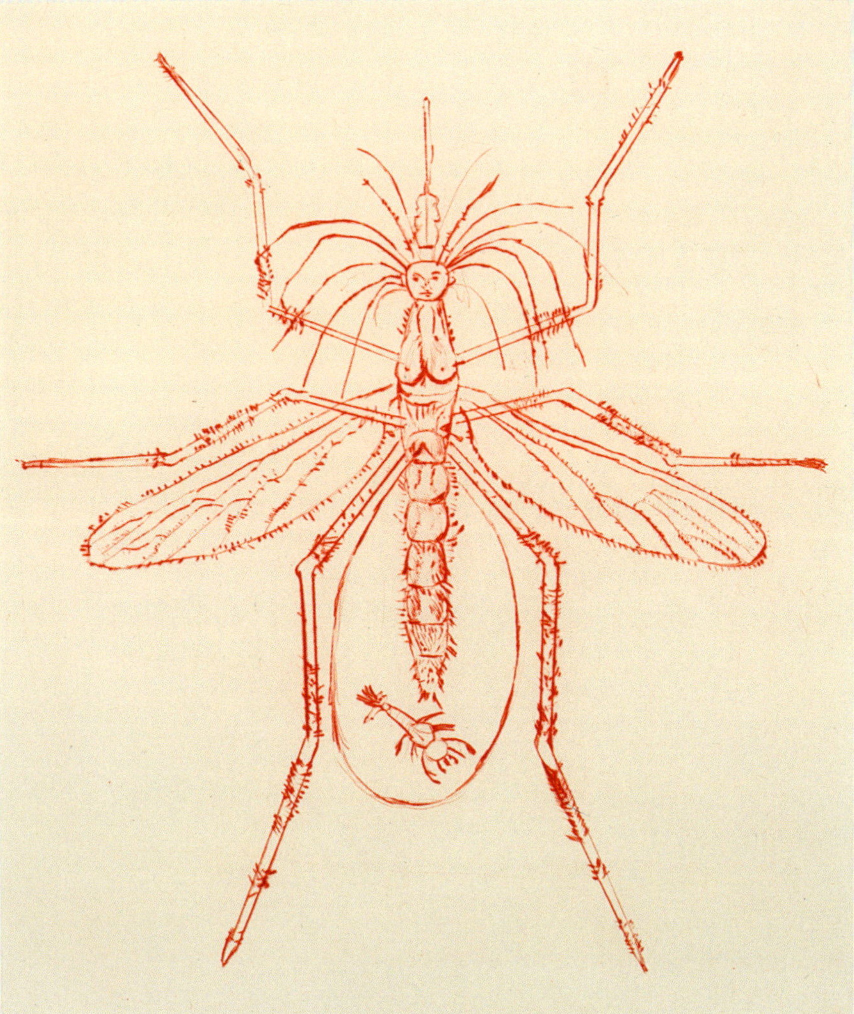

The Smell of the Feet

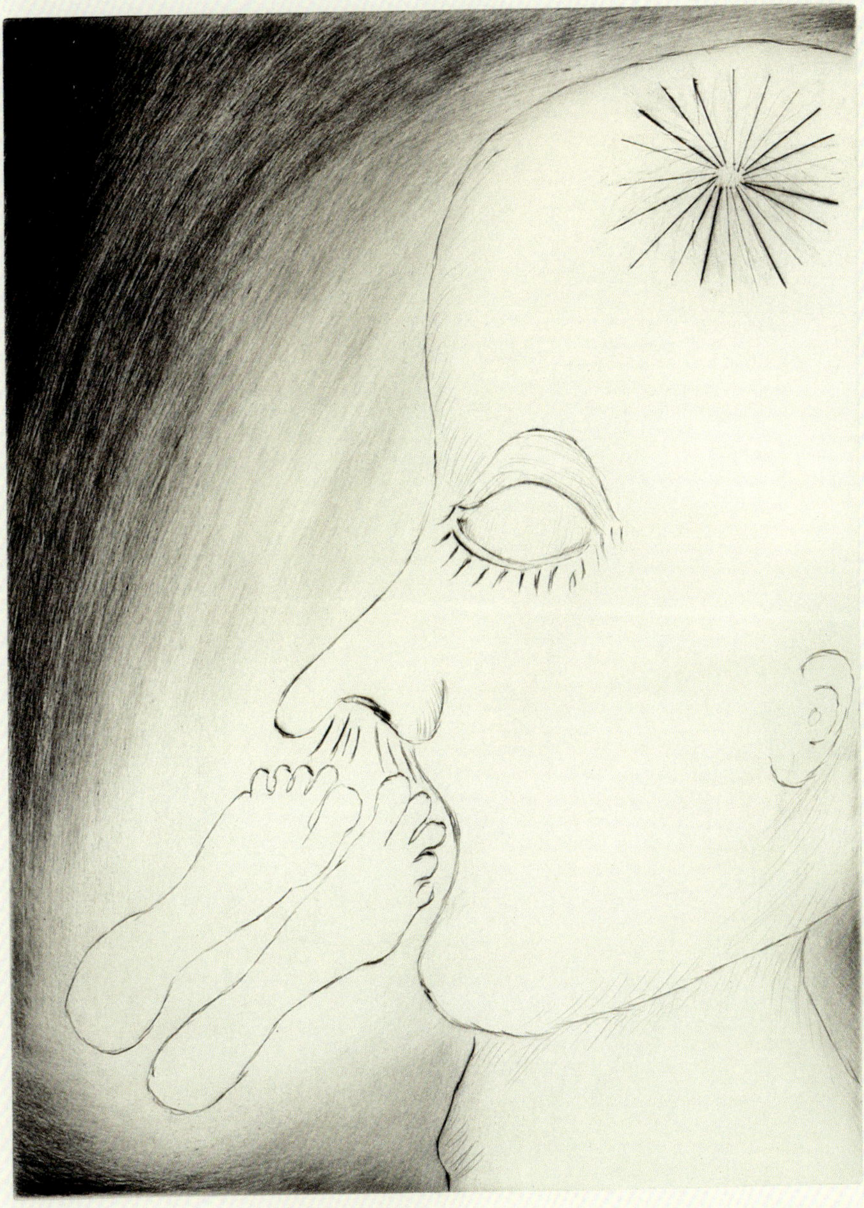

Mother and Child

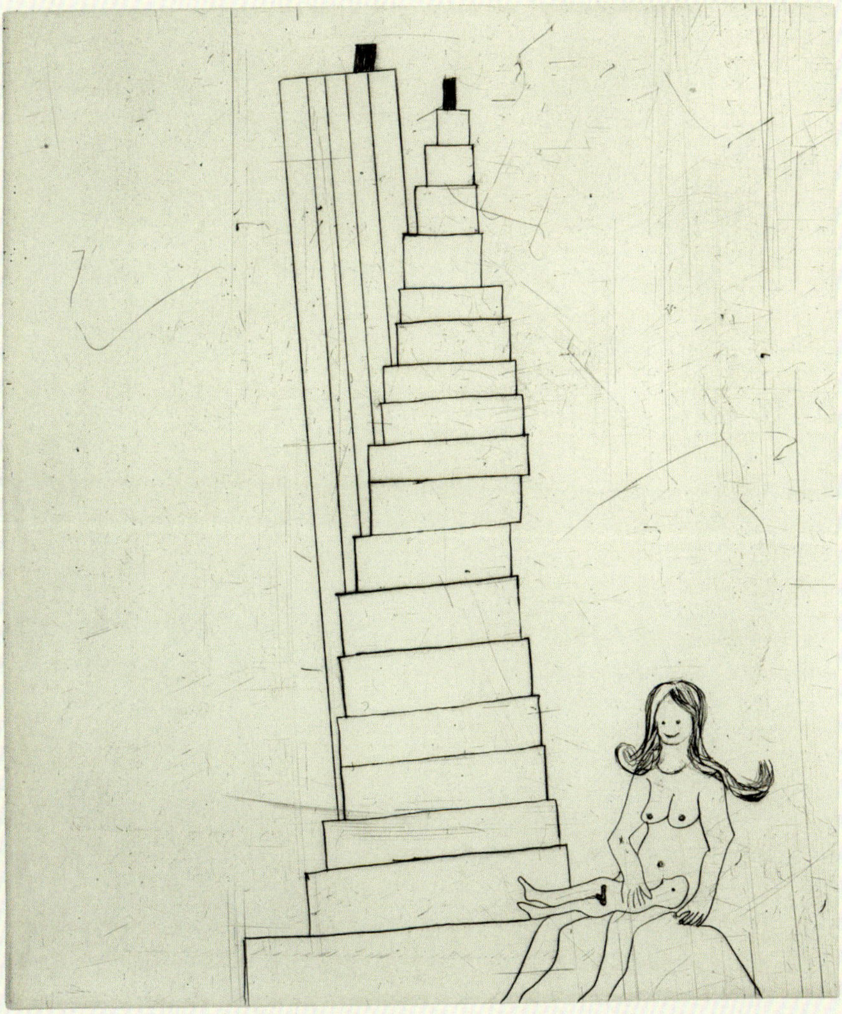

The Angry Cat

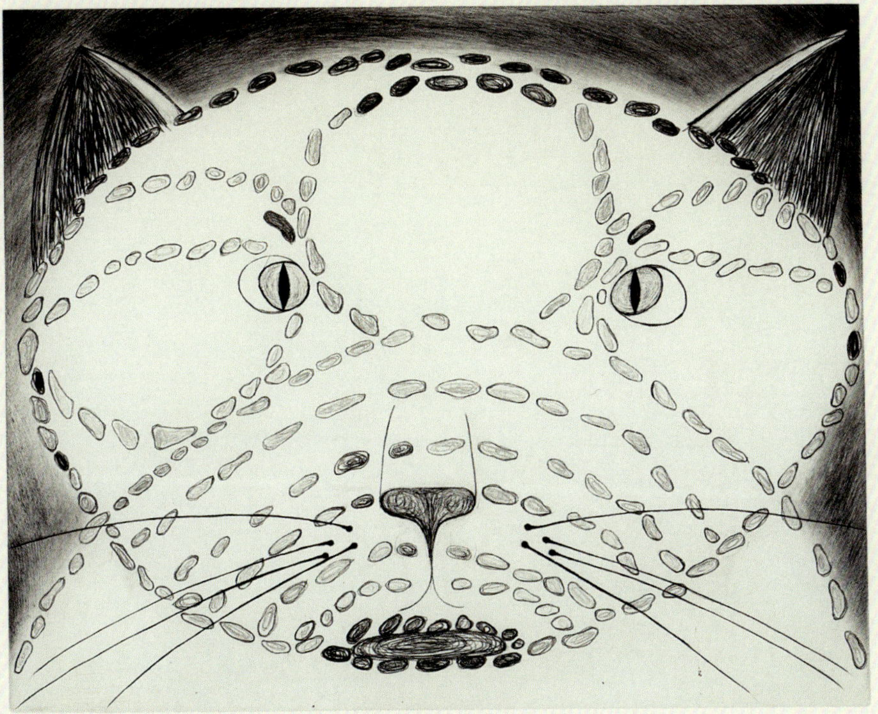

Autobiographical Series

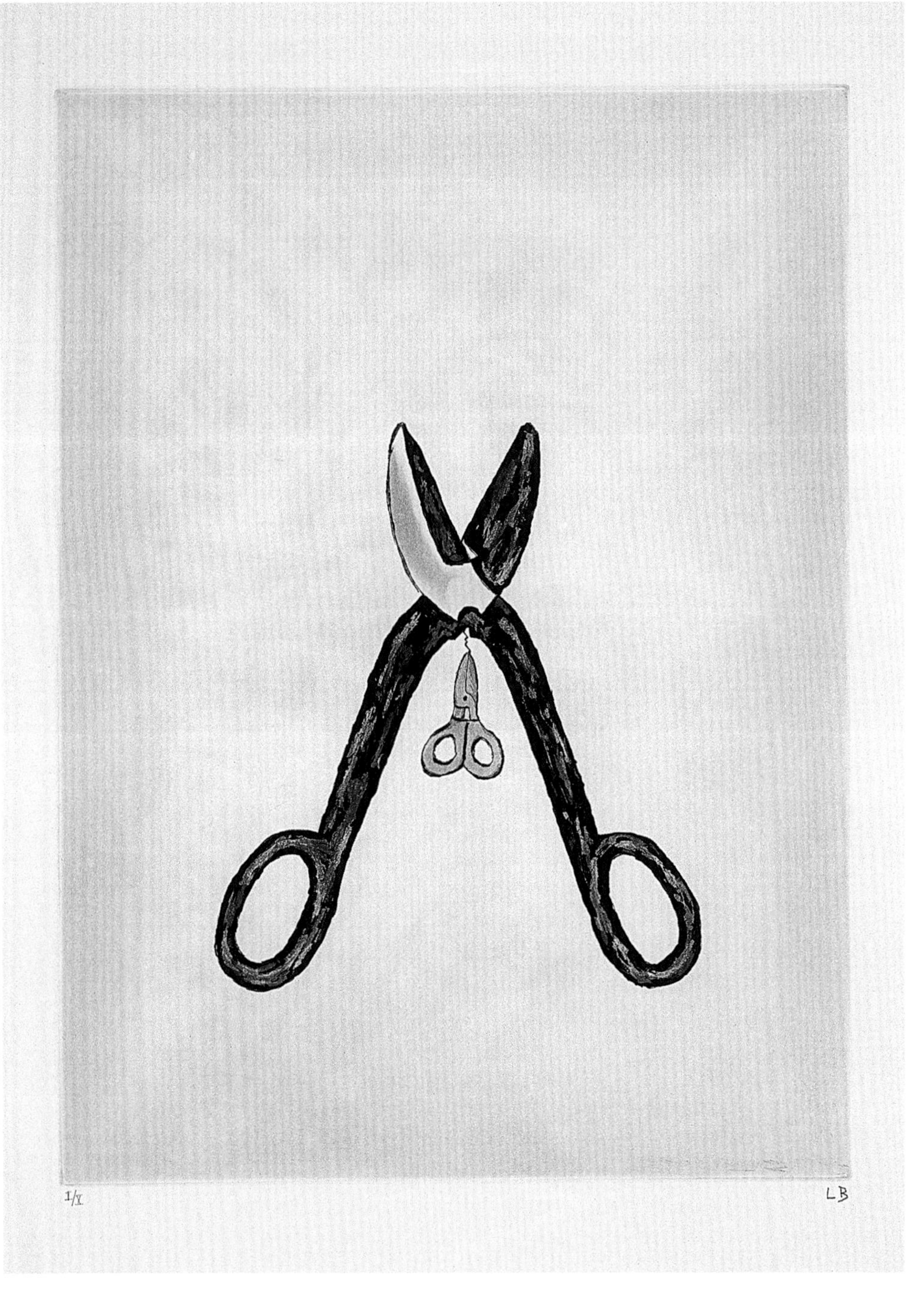

Untitled (Scissors)

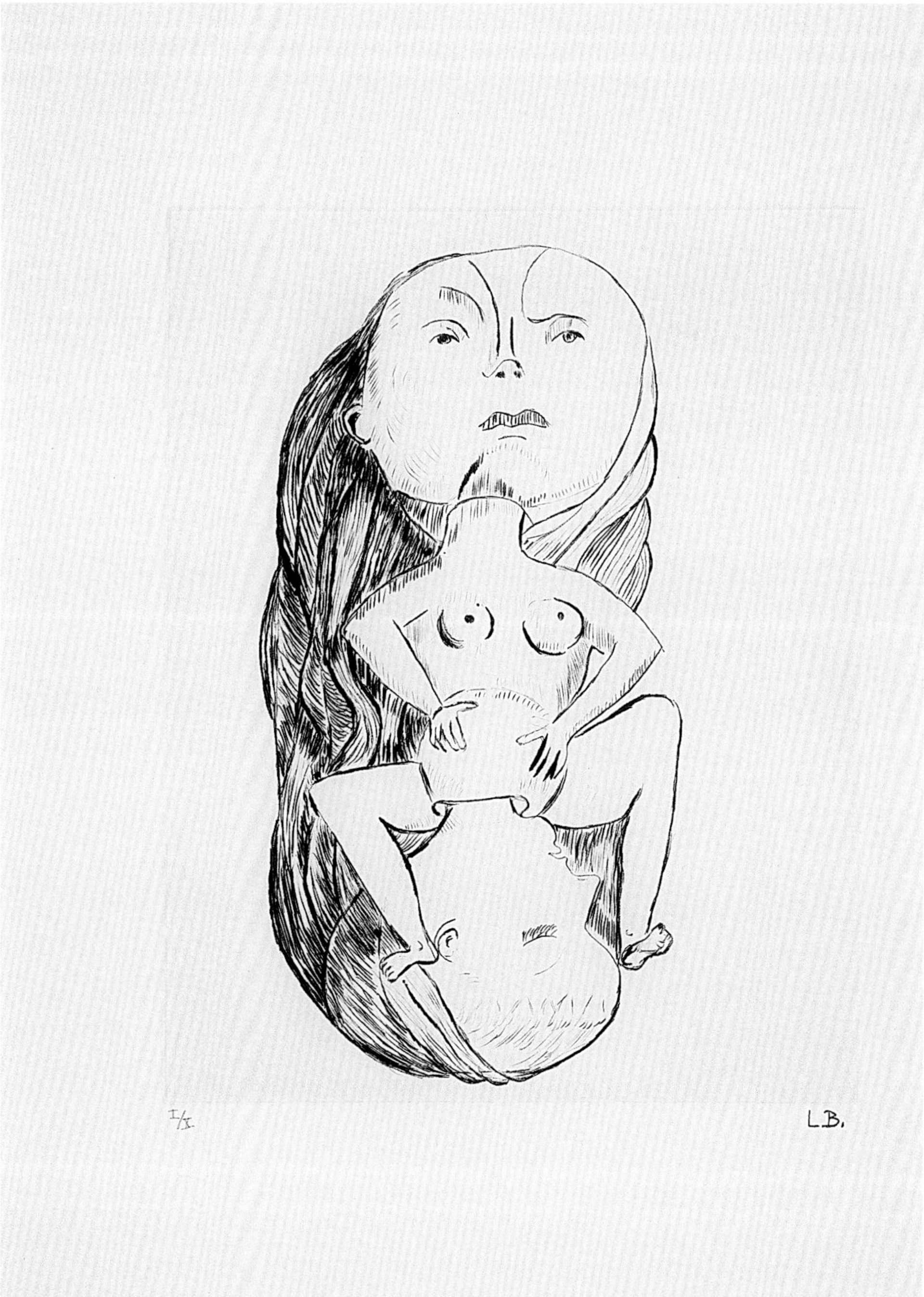

Untitled (Birth)

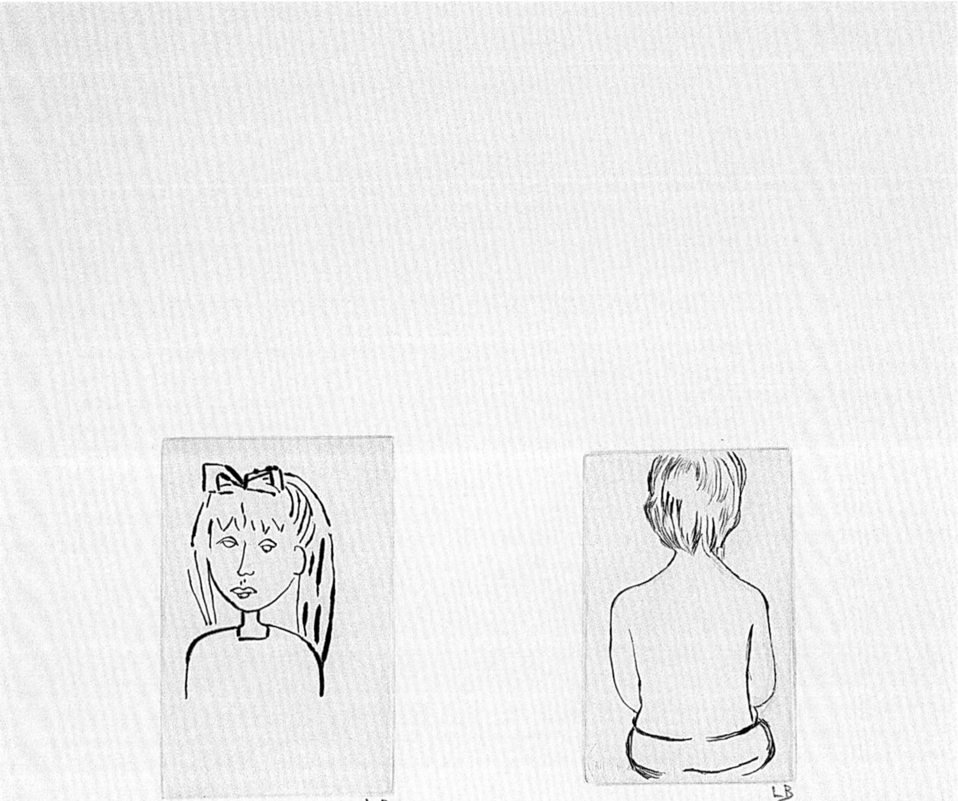

Untitled (Boy and Girl)

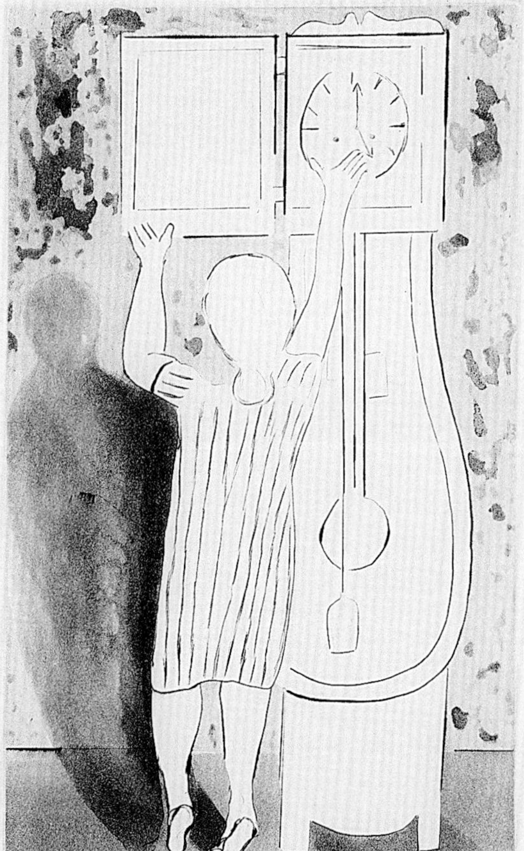

Untitled (Woman and Clock)

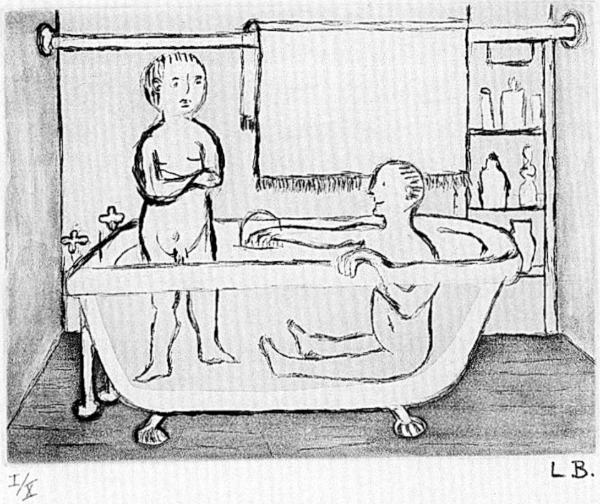

Untitled (Children in Tub)

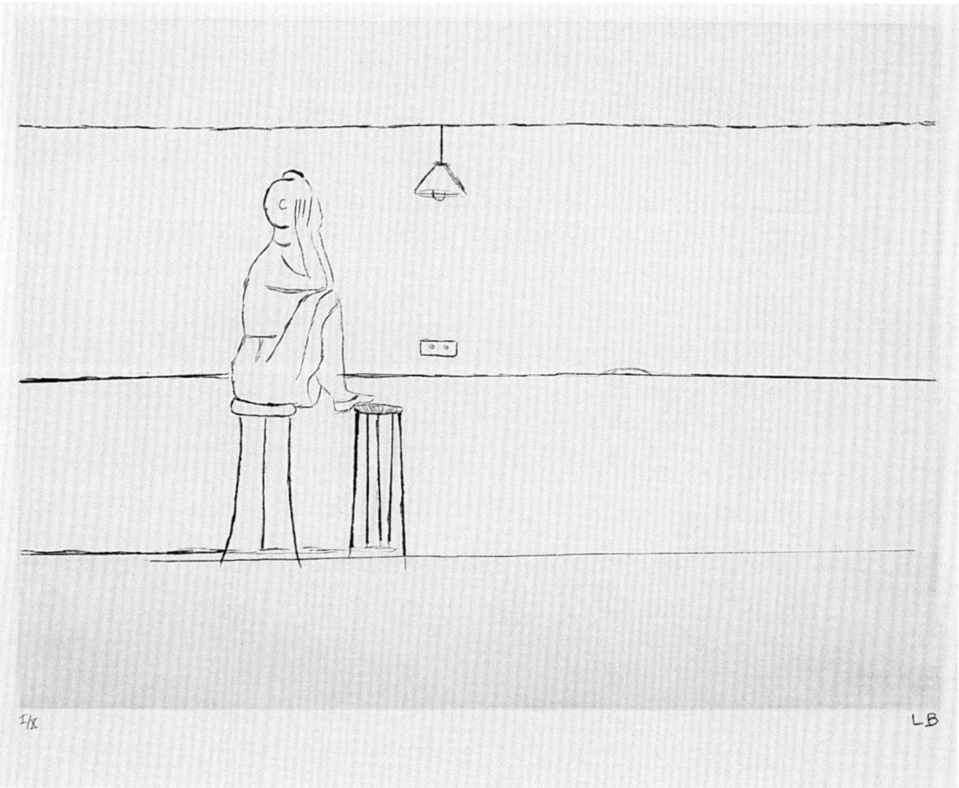
I/X
LB

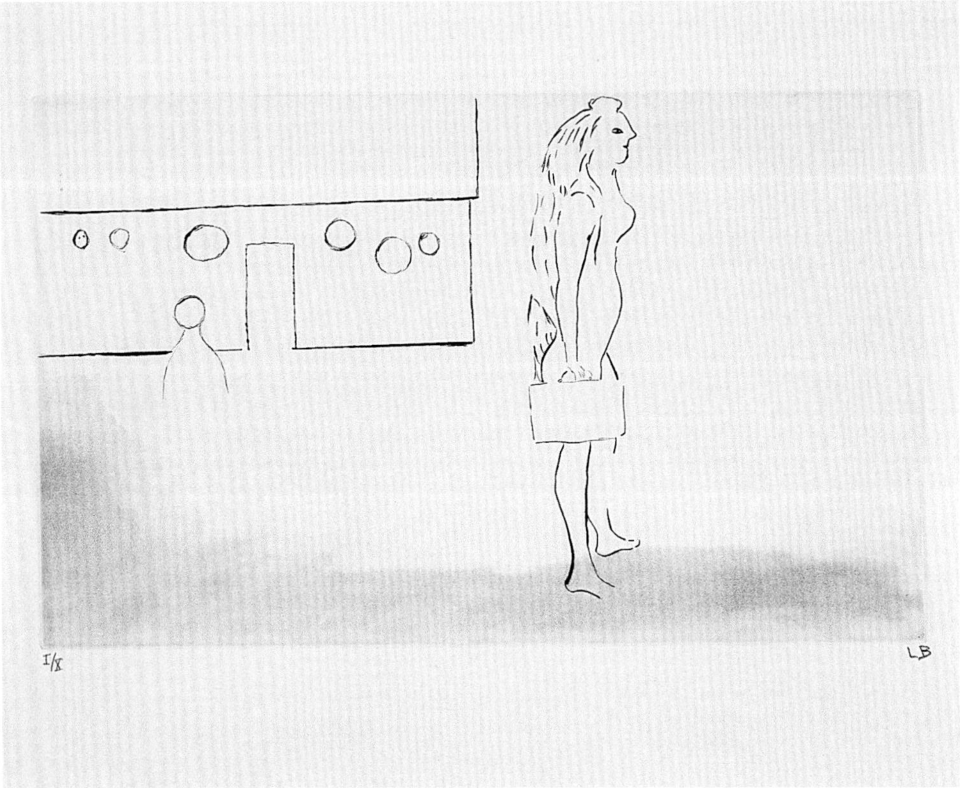

Untitled (Woman with Suitcase)

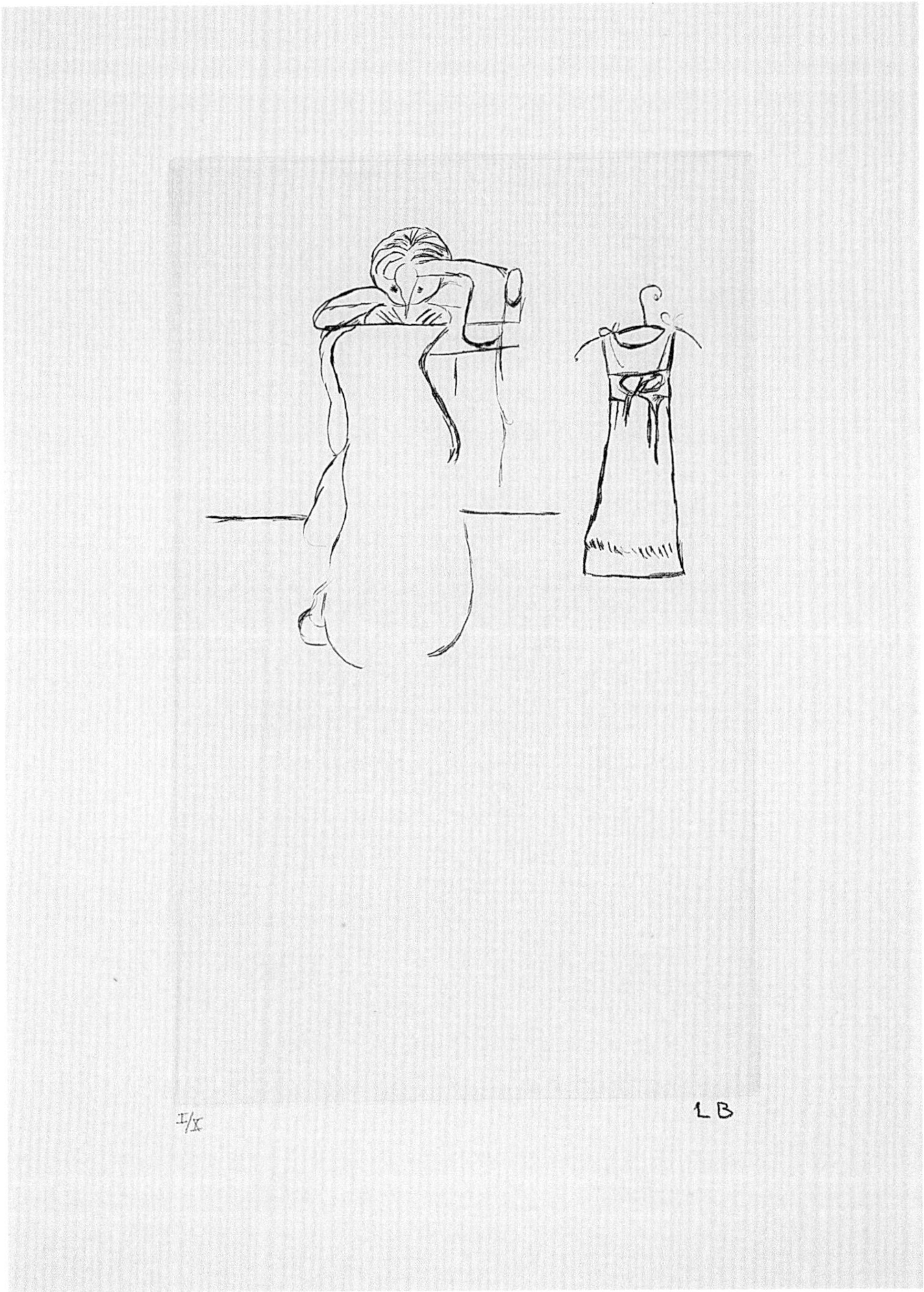

Untitled (Sewing)

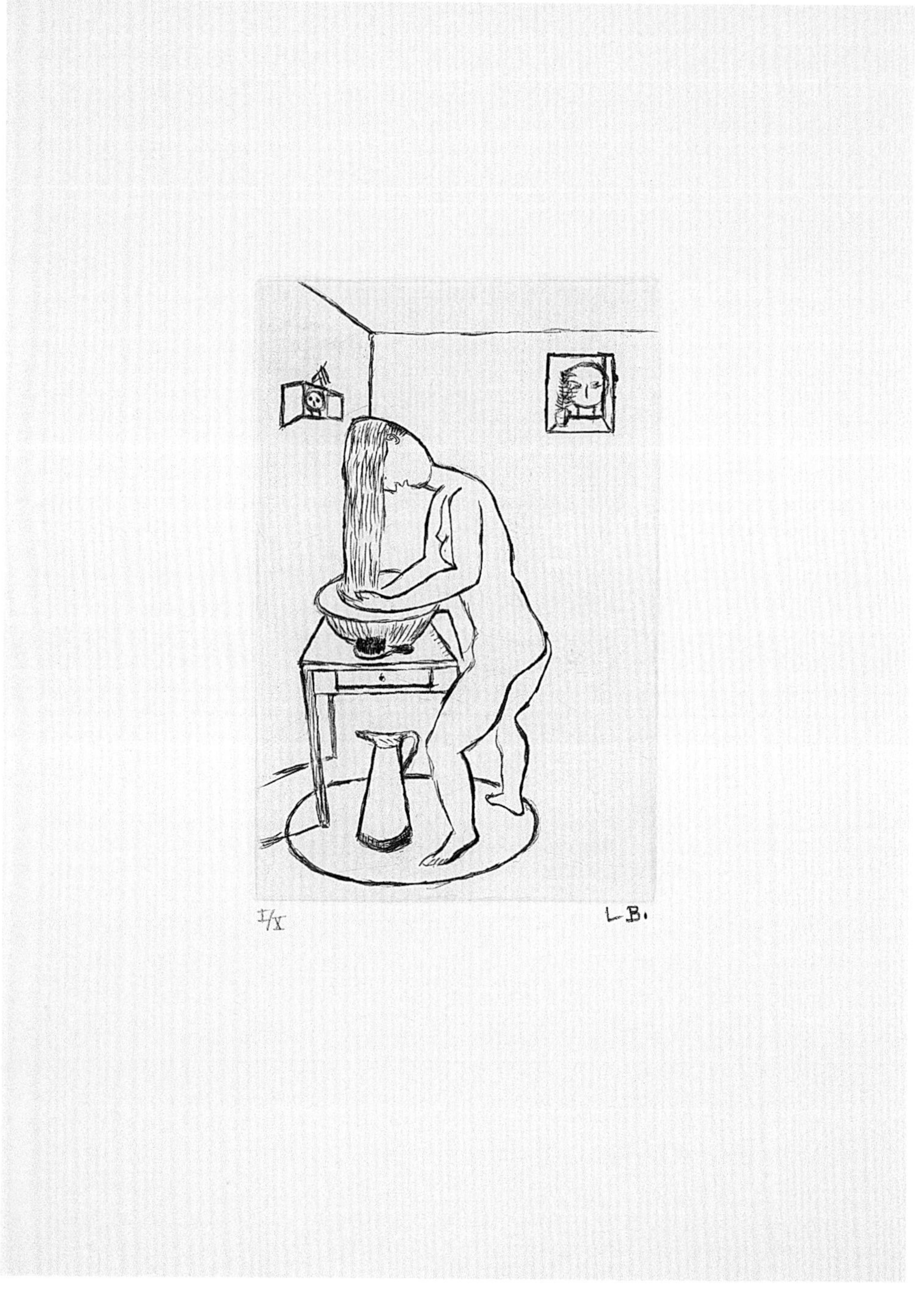

Untitled (Toilette)

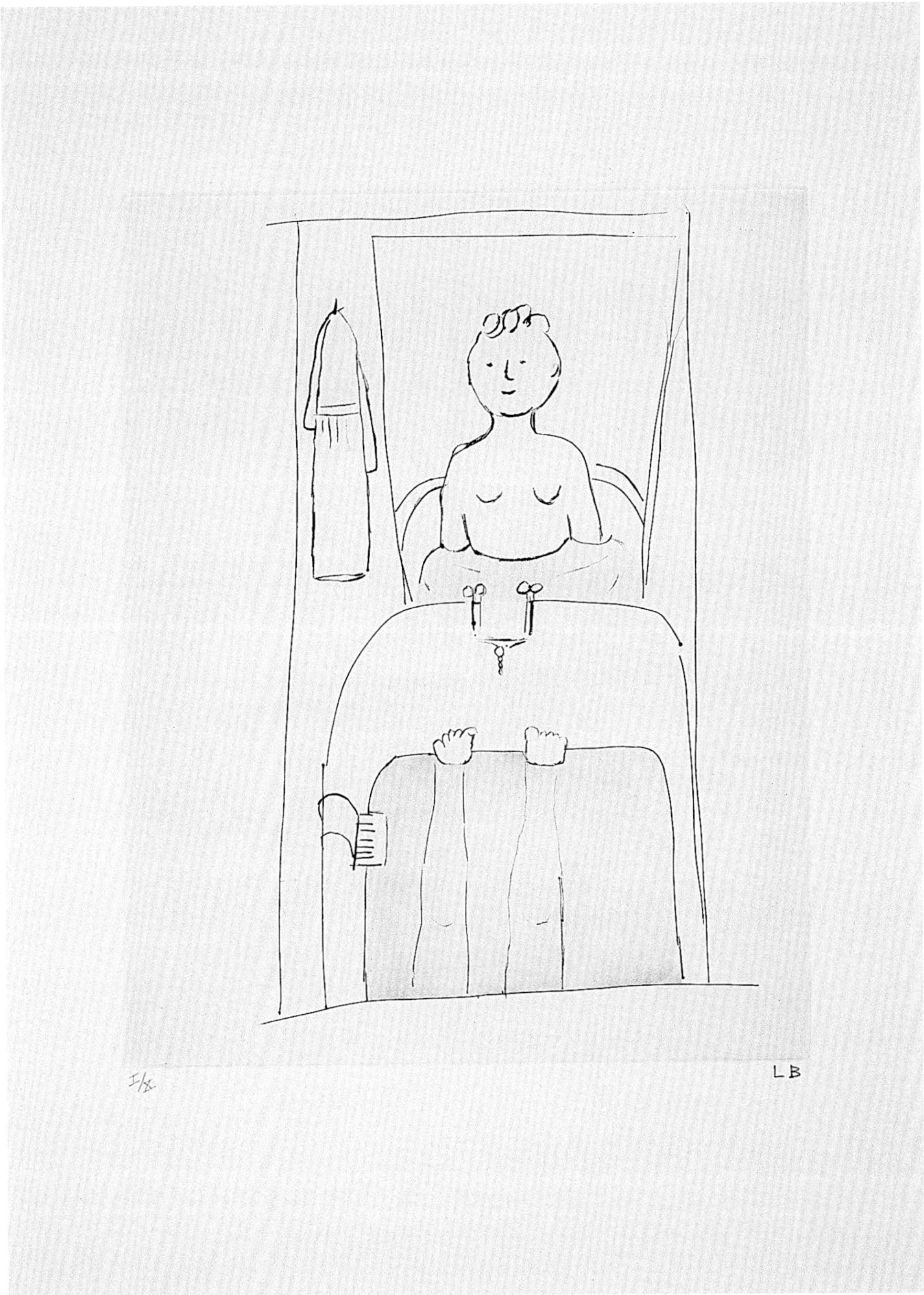

Untitled (Woman in Bathtub)

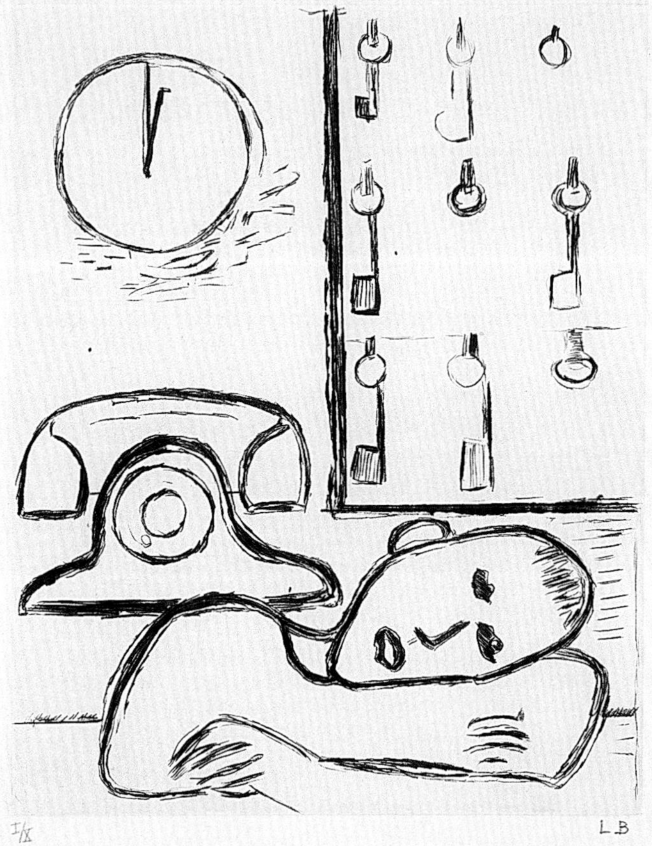

Untitled (Man, Keys, Phone, Clock)

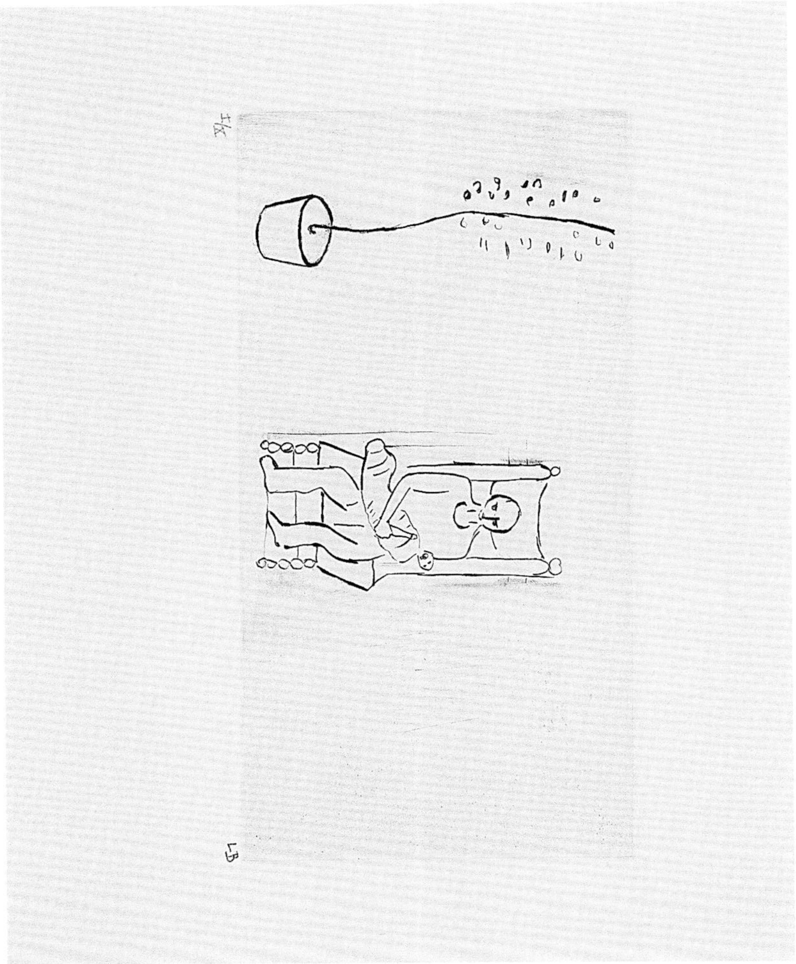

Paternity

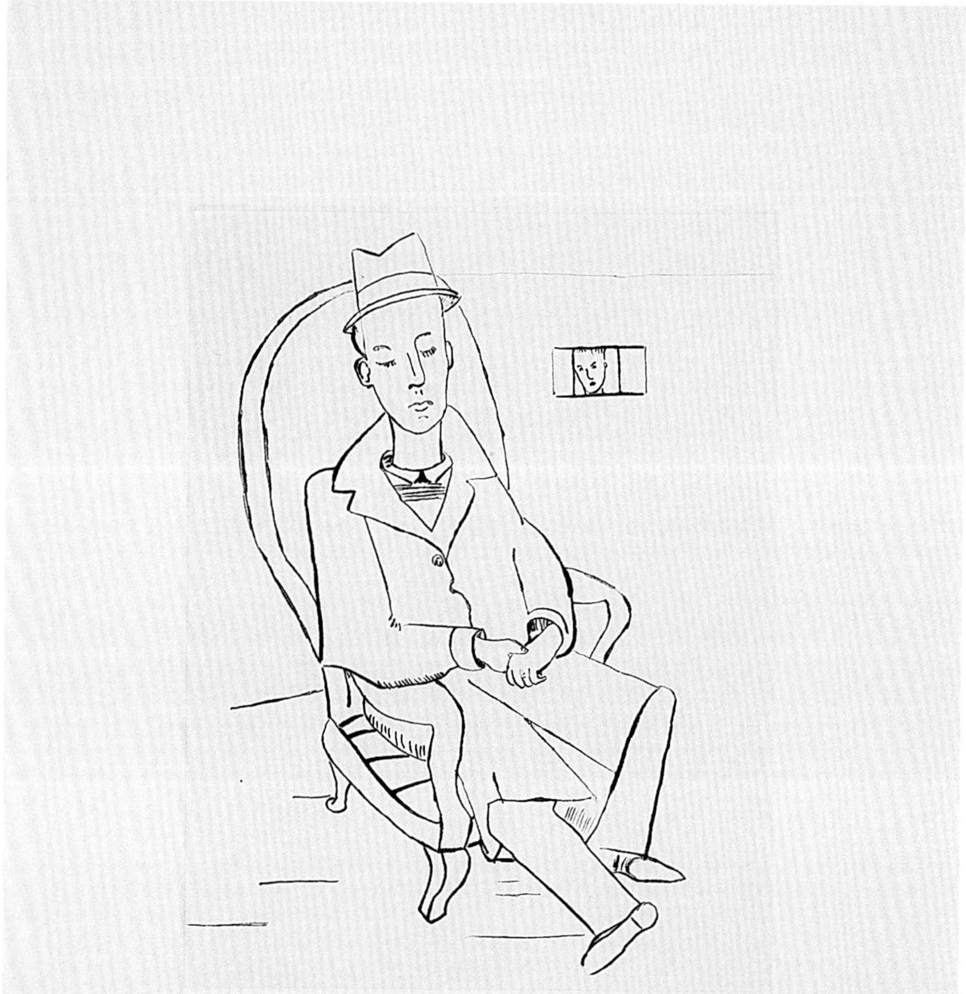

Untitled (Sleeping Man)

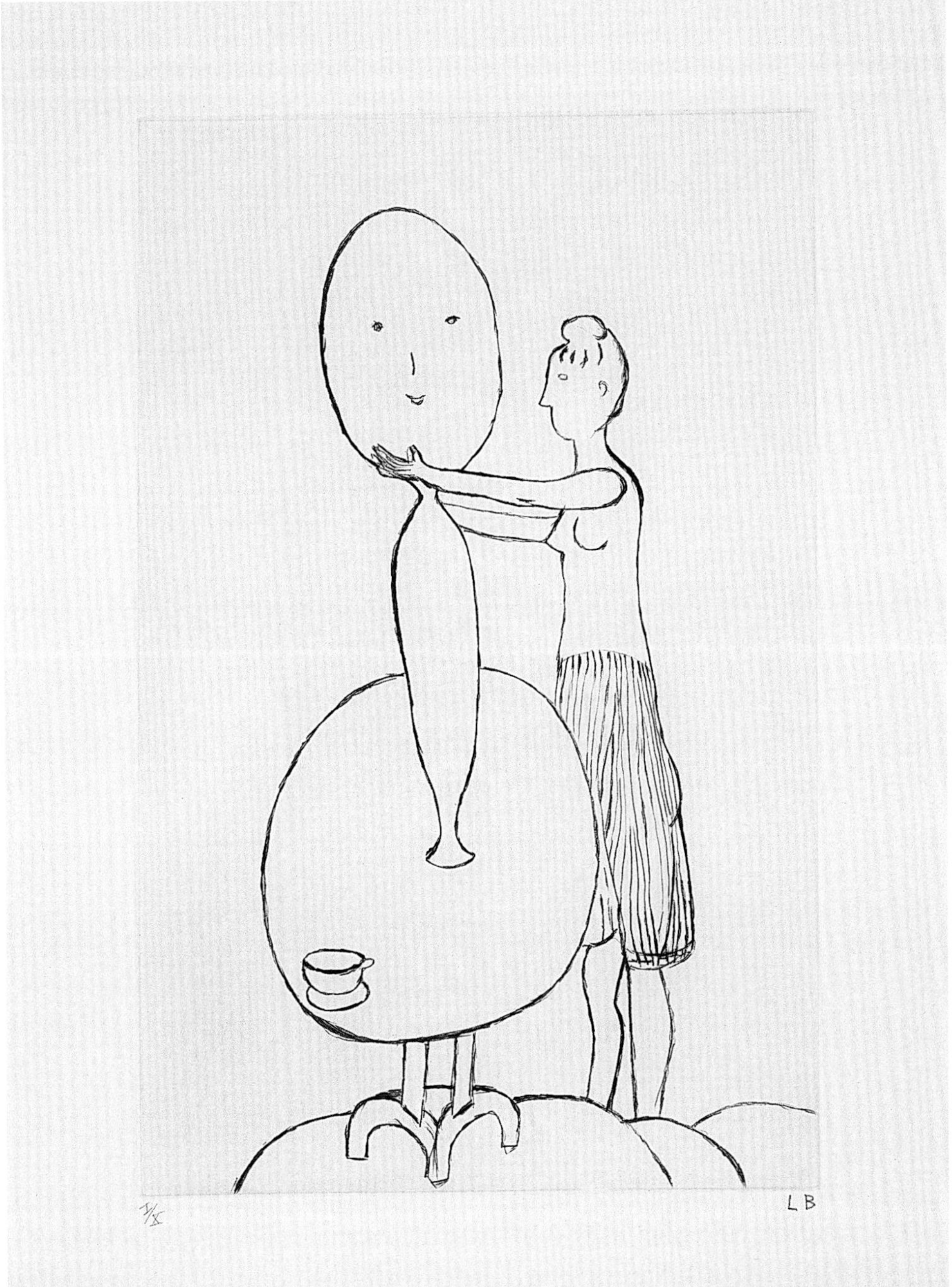

Untitled (Sculptress)

List of Works

11 Drypoints

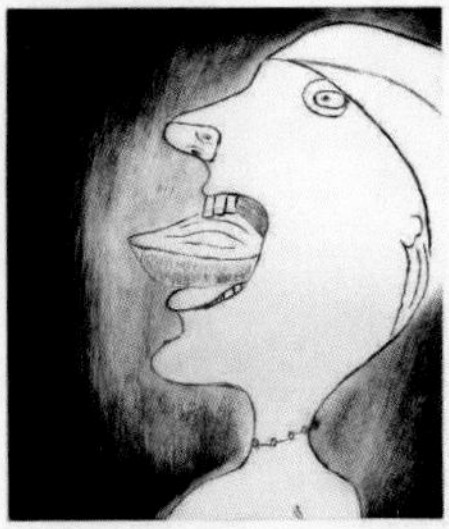

Madeleine, 1999
Drypoint on paper
43.5 × 38.2 cm

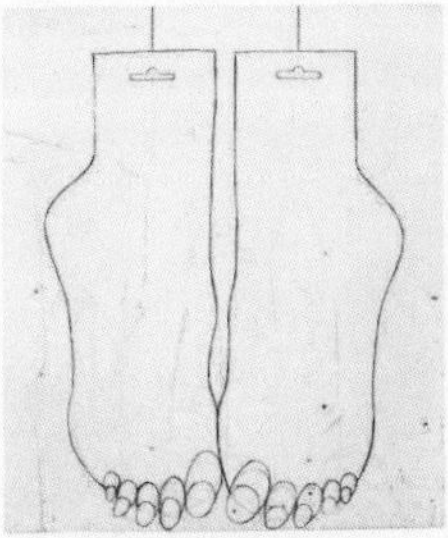

Feet (Socks), 1999
Drypoint on paper
43.5 × 38.2 cm

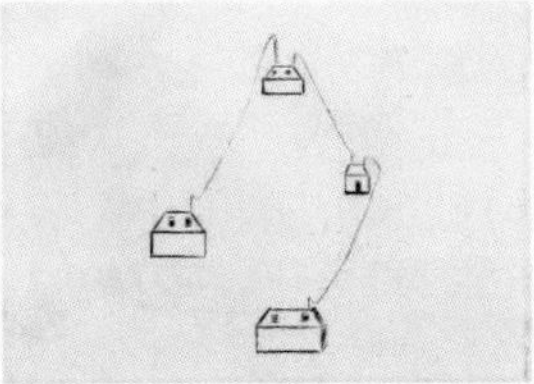

Fences Are Obsolete, 1999
Drypoint on paper
38.2 × 43.5 cm

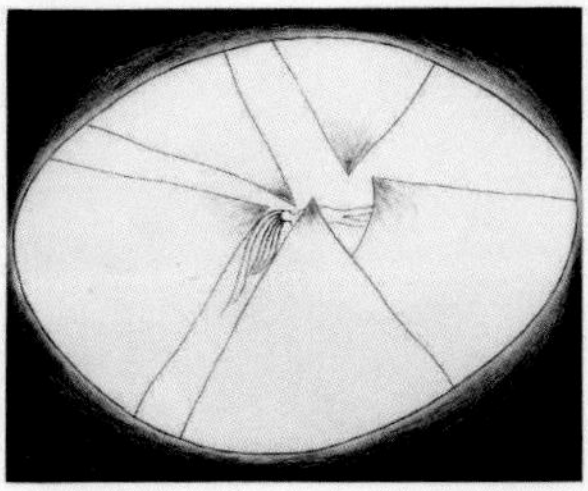

Please Hang in There, 1999
Drypoint on paper
38.2 × 43.5 cm

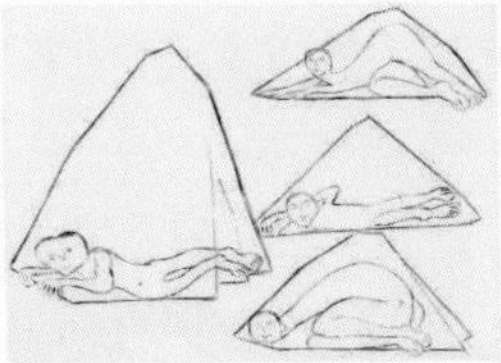

Fear, 1999
Drypoint on paper
38.2 × 43.5 cm

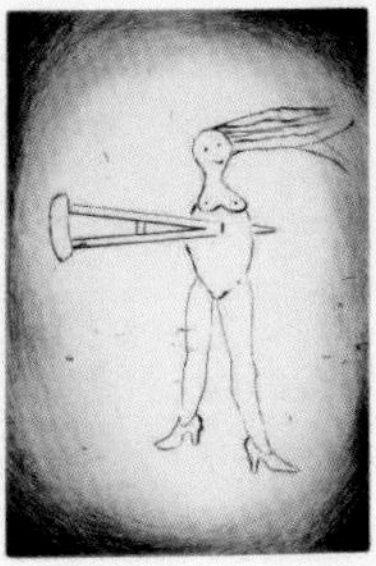

The Accident, 1999
Drypoint on paper
43.5 × 38.2 cm

11 Drypoints

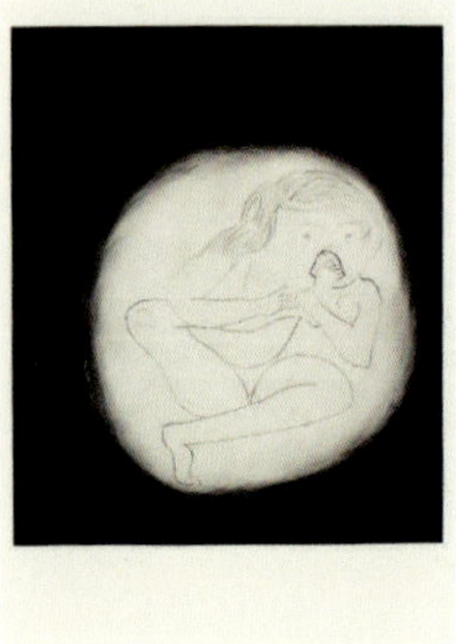

Don't Put Your Foot in Your Mouth, 1999
Drypoint on paper
43.5 × 38.2 cm

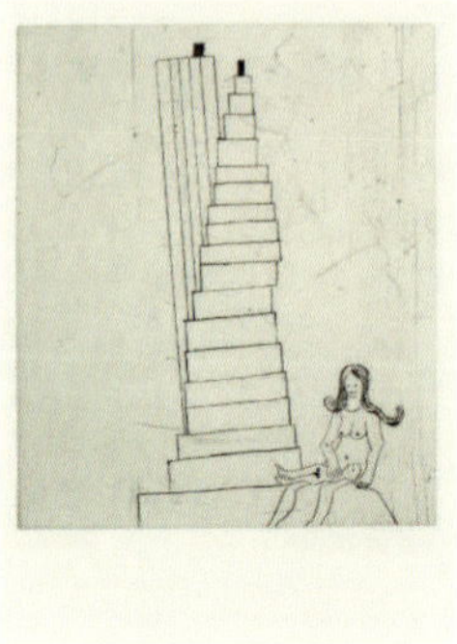

Mother and Child, 1999
Drypoint on paper
43.5 × 38.2 cm

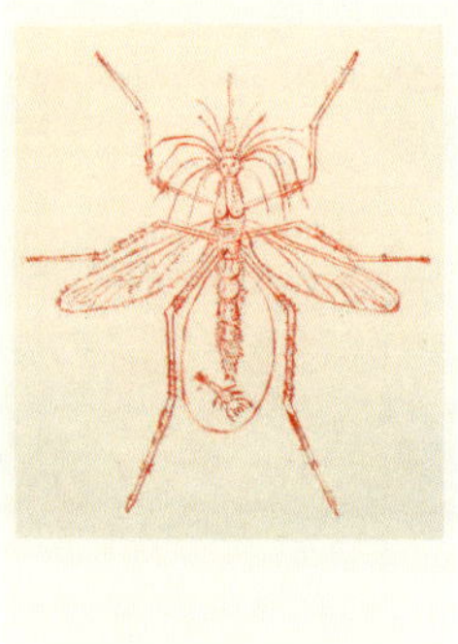

Mosquito, 1999
Drypoint on paper
43.5 × 38.2 cm

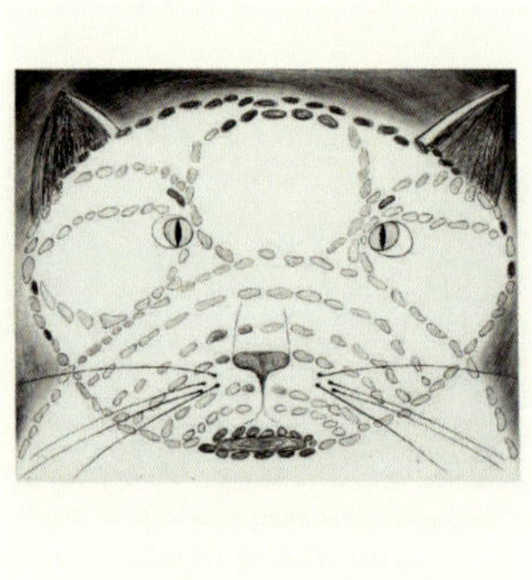

The Angry Cat, 1999
Drypoint on paper
38.2 × 43.5 cm

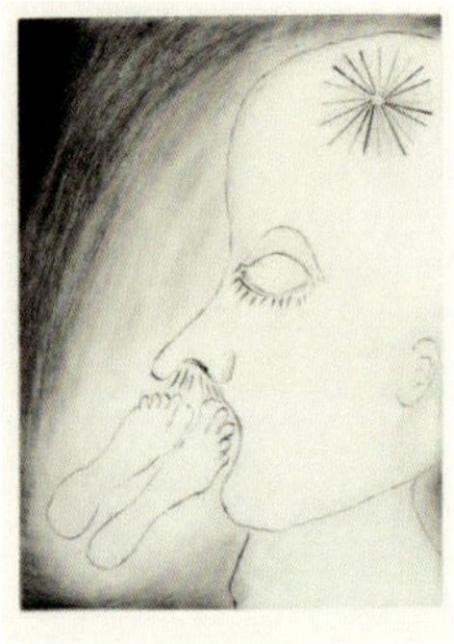

The Smell of the Feet, 1999
Drypoint on paper
43.5 × 38.2 cm

Autobiographical Series

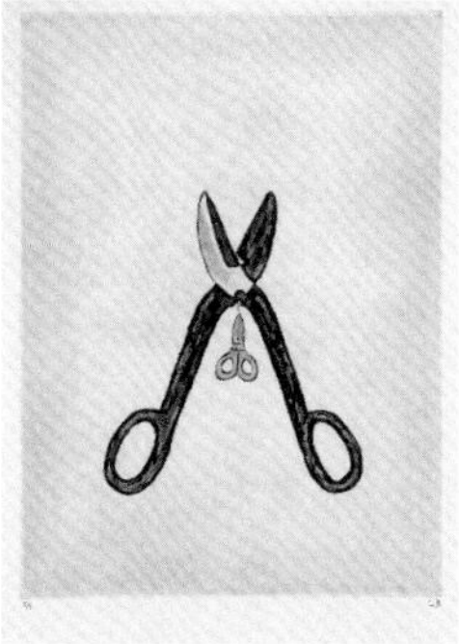

Untitled (Scissors), 1994
Drypoint and aquatint on paper
57 × 38.5 cm

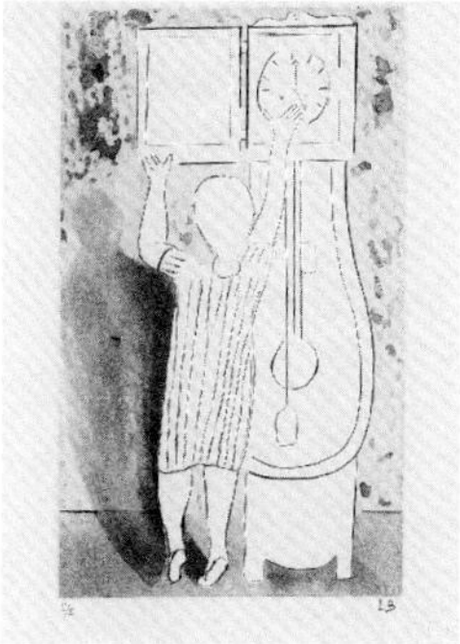

Untitled (Woman and Clock), 1994
Drypoint and aquatint on paper
48.2 × 34.4 cm

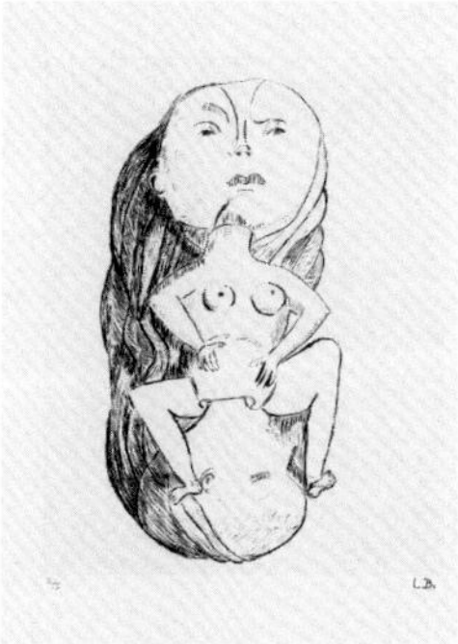

Untitled (Birth), 1994
Drypoint on paper
48.1 × 34.3 cm

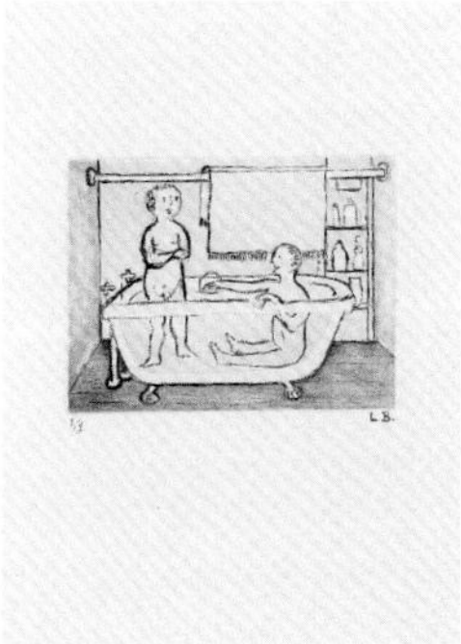

Untitled (Children in Tub), 1994
Drypoint and aquatint on paper
48.1 × 34.3 cm

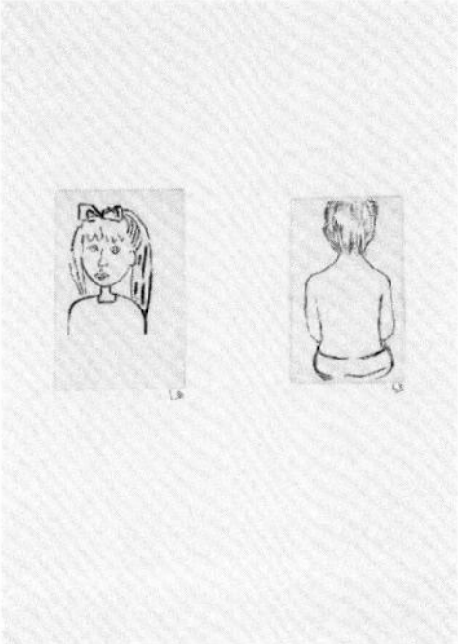

Untitled (Boy and Girl), 1994
Drypoint on paper
50.8 × 38.2 cm

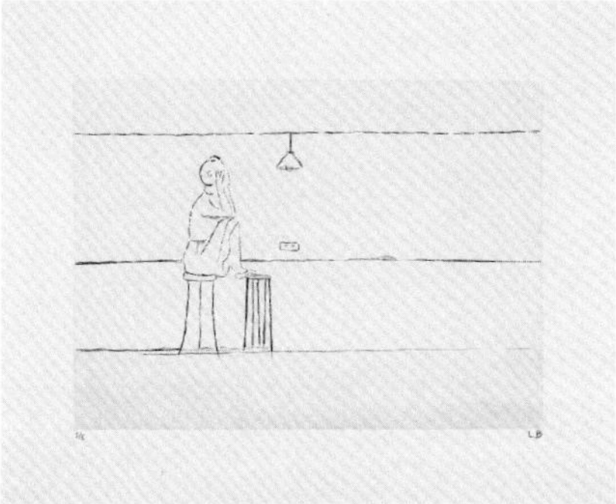

Empty Nest, 1994
Drypoint on paper
38.9 × 53.1 cm

Autobiographical Series

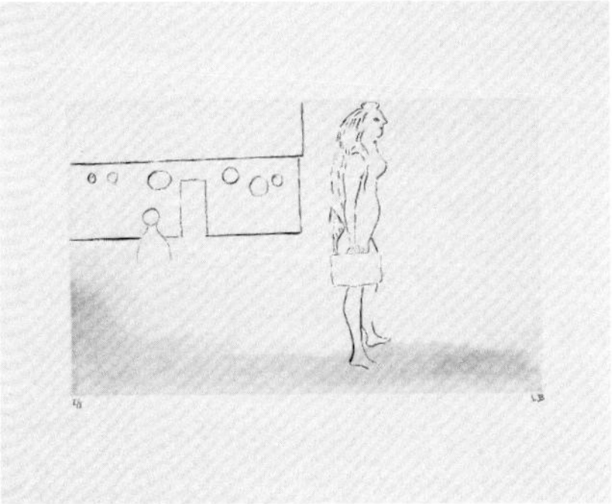

Untitled (Woman with Suitcase), 1994
Drypoint and aquatint on paper
38.7 × 52.9 cm

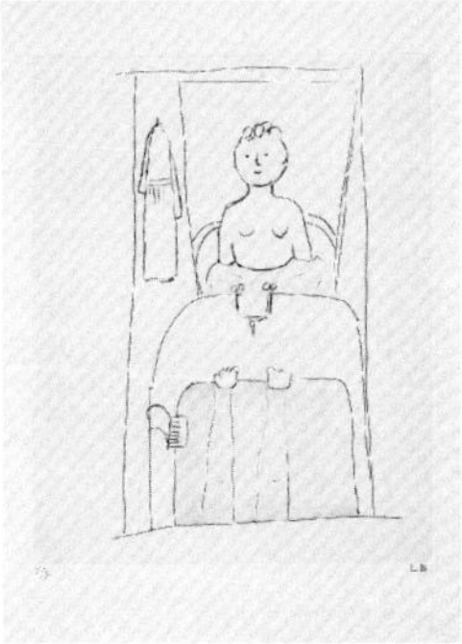

Untitled (Woman in Bathtub), 1994
Drypoint and aquatint on paper
57.1 × 48.4 cm

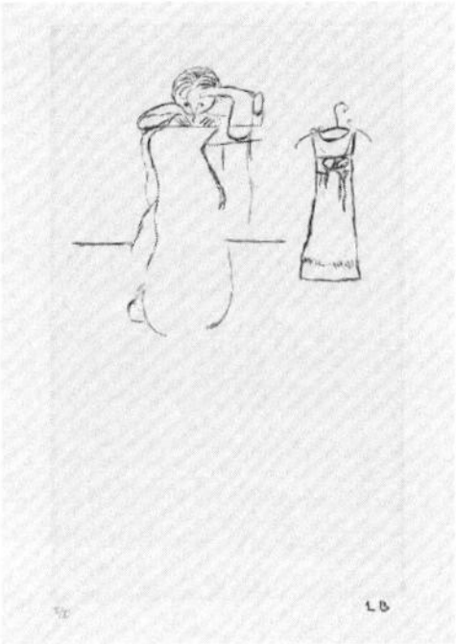

Untitled (Sewing), 1994
Drypoint on paper
41.4 × 29.4 cm

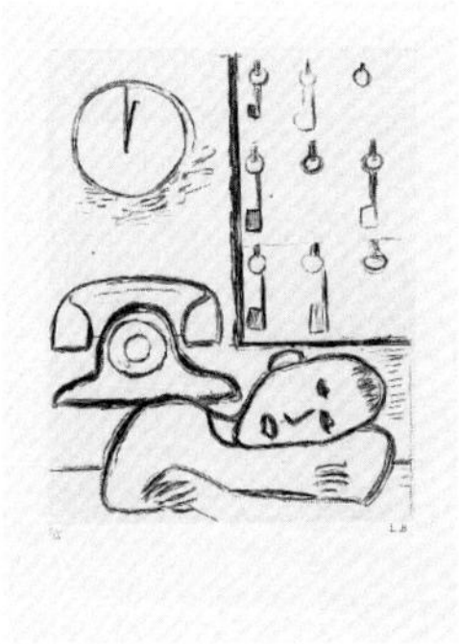

Untitled (Man, Keys, Phone, Clock), 1994
Drypoint on paper
50.7 × 38.1 cm

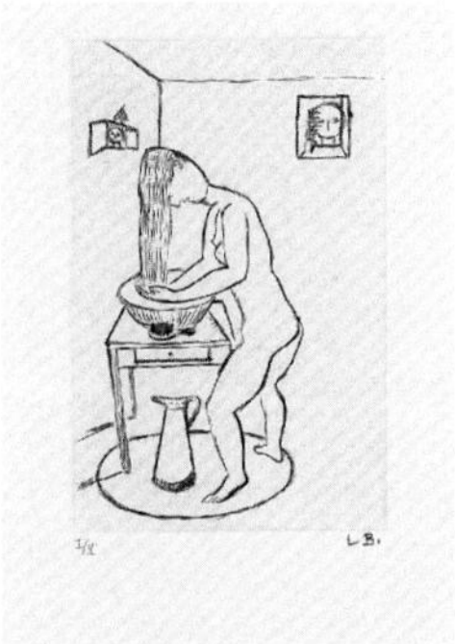

Untitled (Toilette), 1994
Drypoint on paper
41.3 × 29.4 cm

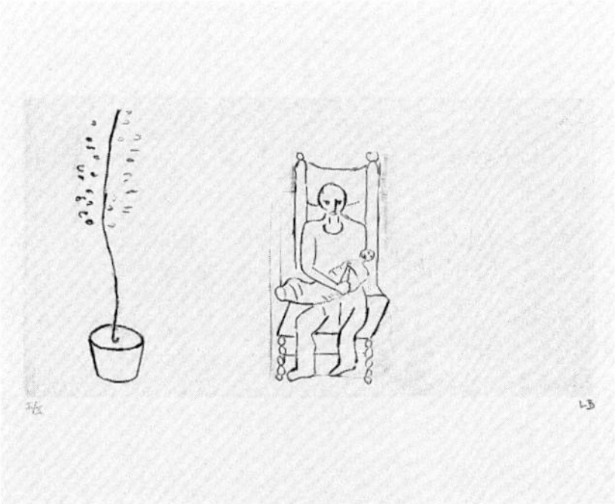

Paternity, 1994
Drypoint on paper
34.2 × 57.4 cm

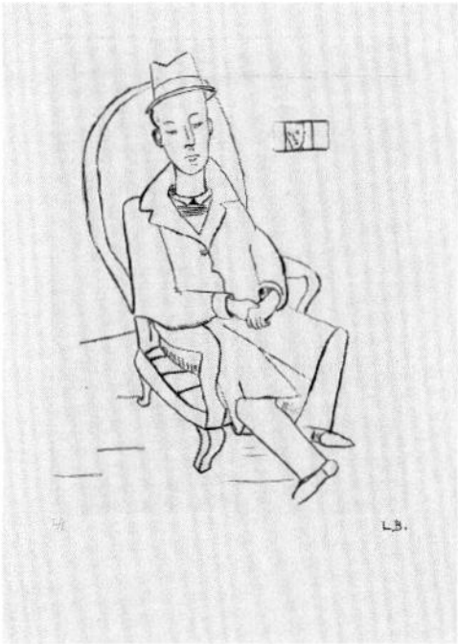

Untitled (Sleeping Man), 1994
Drypoint on paper
50.6 × 38.2 cm

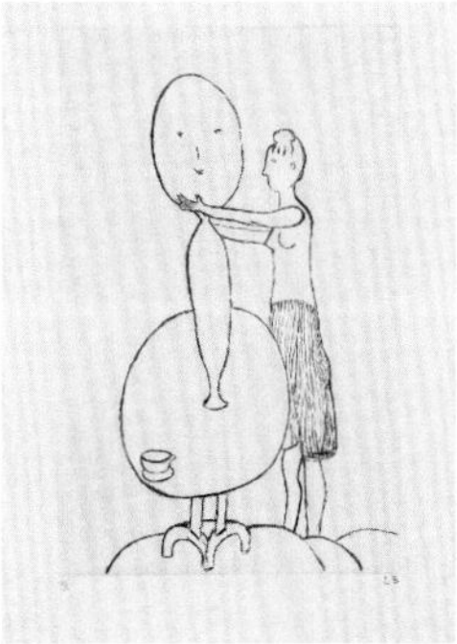

Untitled (Sculptress), 1994
Drypoint on paper
57.1 × 38.2 cm